ICONIC

WOMEN IN

SPORT

CANDI WILLIAMS

summersdale

ICONIC WOMEN IN SPORT

An Hachette UK Company
www.hachette.co.uk

Summersdale Publishers Ltd
Part of Octopus Publishing Group Limited
Carmelite House
50 Victoria Embankment
LONDON
EC4Y 0DZ
UK

www.summersdale.com

Printed and bound in Poland

ISBN: 978-1-78783-563-4

Disclaimer: Facts are correct as of April 2020.

CONTENTS

INTRODUCTION

Run like a girl?
Fight like a girl?
Throw like a girl?

For decades "like a girl" has been used as a demeaning slur when it comes to sporting talk.

Sharing some of the glass-ceiling-shattering stories of incredible sportswomen, this book proves that women are anything but inferior.

It highlights some of the many epic achievements of women sporting icons. Icons who are not just some of the best sportswomen of all time but some of the very best sportspeople of all time.

From Paralympians and Olympians to surfing, soccer and sailing legends, it celebrates the strength, determination, resilience and sheer brilliance of women sporting heroes on land, sand, track, ground and at sea.

Of course, it's by no means an exhaustive list. In fact, whittling it down to just 39 women sporting superheroes was one of the biggest challenges. Lots of these women have paved the way for and been inspired by other incredible women in sports – of whom there are millions!

What this little book should do, however, is give you a snapshot into the many amazing ways that wonder women are kicking ass and breaking down boundaries in the sporting industry, day by day and success by success.

I hope you enjoy and take some inspiration from it.

And next time someone doubts your ability, or makes you feel you are not good enough, come back to this little book and remember you can do absolutely anything you set your mind to.

Never give up x

BABE DIDRIKSON ZAHARIAS

26 June 1911–27 September 1956

HER SUPERPOWERS:

It takes a lot to win an Olympic medal in just one sport – but to do it in three different events is one heck of an achievement. And Babe Didrikson Zaharias had it nailed.

HER INCREDIBLE STORY

Having landed Olympic trophies in three different events, Babe Didrikson Zaharias is known as one of the greatest athletes of all time. Showing amazing athletic skills from a young age, Babe dropped out of school to work for an insurance firm in Dallas purely so she could join the company's esteemed basketball team, the Golden Cyclones. They went on to win the Amateur Athletic Union (AAU) Basketball Championships in 1931, with Babe as their star forward.

In 1932, Babe turned her attention to track and field, and headed for the AAU Championships. All of the other teams were made up of dozens of athletes, while Babe competed as a one-woman team representing her company. She stole the show, taking part in eight events – from hurdles to discus – in three hours. She set records in javelin, 80-m hurdles, high jump and basketball throw and performed brilliantly enough to qualify for five Olympic events.

At the 1932 Los Angeles Olympics, Babe broke four world records. She won gold for javelin with a 43.69-m throw, the 80-m hurdle with a time of 11.7 seconds (breaking her own record in the final) and took home silver for her 1.657-m high jump. The only reason she didn't take on more events is because women were forbidden from competing in more than three at the time.

After an Olympic performance like that, you'd forgive Babe for putting her feet up and carb-loading for a bit. But she didn't sit back. Instead, she took up a new sport: golf. In 1935, she won her first tournament (the Texas Women's Amateurs) and became the first woman to compete against men in the Los Angeles Open tournament in 1938.

Babe's dedication to golf was limitless and her self-confidence unwavering. She'd passionately drive as many as 1,000 balls a day, taking lessons for six hours at a time until her hands were bleeding. She went on to set records in the PGA Tour events and won the 1946 US Women's Amateur, the 1947 British Ladies Amateur (as the first American to do so) and three Women's Western Opens as an amateur. After turning pro, she won over 30 championships and tournaments. She bravely competed for her final trophies while battling terminal colon cancer, playing golf even when fitted with a colostomy bag.

Babe's incredible success didn't come without scrutiny. She faced a lot of jibes from the press who, back then, largely believed that women were better placed preparing supper courses than playing on golf courses. When asked how she managed to hit 238-m tee shots, Babe simply replied "I just loosen my girdle and let [the ball] fly." Words of wisdom!

HER AWESOME ACHIEVEMENTS

→ The only person ever to receive individual trophies in hurdle, jump and throwing events in one Olympics.

→ As the 1932 Olympics was the first time women's javelin had been included, Babe was the first ever female Olympic javelin champion.

→ Founding member of the Ladies Professional Golf Association (LPGA), which she helped set up in 1950.

→ Received the Bob Jones Award posthumously – the highest honour given by the United States Golf Association.

"THE FORMULA FOR SUCCESS IS SIMPLE: PRACTICE AND CONCENTRATION, THEN MORE PRACTICE AND MORE CONCENTRATION."

BILLIE JEAN KING

22 November 1943–present

HER SUPERPOWERS:

The King who is a total tennis queen. Before Serena and Venus, there was the legend of Billie Jean.

HER INCREDIBLE STORY

Equality advocate and six-time women's world champion Billie Jean has earned her place in history as one of the greatest tennis players of all time.

Billie Jean set her ambitions high from an early age. At just eleven years old, she saved up $8 from odd jobs to buy her first racket. She played endlessly on the free courts of her hometown in Long Beach and took advantage of any freebie lessons going.

Billie Jean soon noticed the rules were different for female and male players. In her first tournament in 1955, she was barred from a team photo for wearing tennis shorts her mother had made her, rather than the traditional tennis skirt. Instead of letting this dampen her ambition, Billie became an activist for gender equality. Billie Jean campaigned tirelessly for equal prize money for men and women during the early years of the Open Era (when amateurs and professionals started to compete against each other). When she won the 1972 US Open and was paid less than the men's champion, Billie Jean refused to compete in the tournament again unless the prize money was equal. In 1973, the US Open became the first major tournament to offer an equal prize to men and women.

But Billie Jean wasn't campaigning just for herself – she was fighting for all female tennis players. It was this tennis legend who spearheaded the

Women's Tennis Association (WTA) in 1973, to create a better future for female tennis players. Now, the association has over 2,500 players right across the world who compete for $146 million in prize money.

Her quest for parity between the sexes wasn't welcomed by all with open arms. Bobby Riggs, a leading men's player in the 1930s and 1940s and self-confessed chauvinist, claimed that the women's tennis game was "inferior" to the men's. So, 29-year-old Billie Jean did what any awesome female tennis player would do and took 55-year-old Riggs on in a tennis match. She won 6–4, 6–3, 6–3 and took home $100,000. It became the most watched tennis match of all time and is considered a huge stepping stone for women's tennis.

Billie Jean King continued to win championships until she retired in 1990. She became one of the first prominent female sportspeople to come out as gay in 1981, when her relationship with her secretary went public, and it was met with huge controversy. While her tennis career might have ended, her fight for equality and LGBTQ rights lives on. Billie Jean now directs not-for-profit leadership initiatives that aim to break down barriers and promote diverse, inclusive leadership in the workforce.

HER AWESOME ACHIEVEMENTS

→ First female athlete to earn more than US $100,000 in prize money in a single season, in any sport (1972).

→ Between 1961 and 1979, Billie won a staggering 39 Grand Slam titles, including a record 20 Wimbledon titles.

→ First female "Sportsperson of the Year" as chosen by *Sports Illustrated* in 1972.

→ Appointed Global Mentor for Gender Equality by UNESCO (United Nations Educational, Scientific and Cultural Organization) in 2008.

→ One of the first people ever to be inducted into the National Gay and Lesbian Sports Hall of Fame (2013).

"DON'T LET ANYONE DEFINE YOU. YOU DEFINE YOURSELF."

BONNIE BLAIR

18 MARCH 1969–PRESENT

HER SUPERPOWERS:

On ice skates from the age of two and going on to win an Olympic gold at 22, Bonnie Blair is an ice queen and one of the most decorated athletes in Olympic history.

HER INCREDIBLE STORY

Speed skating on ice is no mean feat, especially when you're four years old, as Bonnie Blair was when she first took to the ice competitively.

Coming from a family of great skaters, Bonnie was barely out of school when she landed her place on the US speed-skating team. At 1.65 m, she wasn't as tall as your average skater, but that didn't stop her from giving a flawless performance. Her coach, Cathy Priestner (Olympic silver-medal speed skater), saw potential and encouraged Bonnie to take part in fast-paced long-track races as well as the short-track, pack-style races she'd competed in before.

Bonnie took her first try at Olympic success at just 16. She performed in the trials for the 1980 Winter Olympics but didn't quite make the team. Rather than putting her ambitions on ice, this only inspired Bonnie to work harder for the 1984 Winter Olympics. Alongside raising funds for her training and drumming up support in her local town, Cornwall, New York, Bonnie started training more intensely, including a stint with the US men's team. She made the cut for the 1984 Winter Olympics in Sarajevo and came eighth in the 500-m race.

Despite not landing a medal, Bonnie didn't give up. She took her routine up a notch, adding running, cycling and weightlifting to her daily efforts. Her dedication was worth it. Bonnie won the 1986 short-track world championship and set her first long-track world record in the 500 m in 1987.

She landed her long-awaited Olympic Gold in 1988, winning the 500 m (with a record of 39.1 seconds). It's no easy race, skating competitively in packs with athletes from across the world and, with no height advantage, Bonnie had only her technique and tenacity to rely on. Her signature stroke was super smooth and she used a low crouch to help her, quite literally, glide through the pack. It was this stellar performance that earned her the nickname "Bonnie the Blur".

After her initial win, Bonnie raised hopes for America's future performance in speed skating – and she didn't disappoint. Bonnie skated in four Olympics in total, winning five gold medals and one bronze. She retired (on a high) in 1995, winning gold in the Milwaukee World Championships Sprint.

As a ground-breaking Winter Olympics American athlete who refused to give up on her dream, it was only right that Bonnie carried the Olympic flame when the games returned to the States in 2002. Today she inspires off the ice, working as a director of the US speed-skating board, a motivational speaker and a fundraiser for the American Cancer Society and Alzheimer's Association.

HER AWESOME ACHIEVEMENTS

→ First American woman to win five Olympic gold medals and the first American Winter Olympian to win six career medals.

→ In 1993, Bonnie became the first ever winter athlete to win the Sullivan Award, one of the highest honours for an amateur athlete.

→ Won the World Cup points championship 11 times in total.

→ Awarded a star on the Flag for Hope in 2015 for her outstanding speed-skating career and philanthropic efforts.

"WINNING DOESN'T ALWAYS MEAN BEING FIRST. WINNING MEANS YOU'RE DOING BETTER THAN YOU'VE EVER DONE BEFORE."

CANDACE PARKER

19 April 1986–PRESENT

HER SUPERPOWERS:

The first ever woman to dunk in an NCAA tournament and one of the most decorated basketball players of all time, it's the slam dunkin' superstar Candace Parker.

HER INCREDIBLE STORY

In just a couple of decades, Candace Parker has become a WNBA (Women's National Basketball Association) legend, scooping more than 20 prestigious awards. But, despite coming from a family of basketball royalty (former NBA player Anthony Parker is her brother), basketball wasn't always Candace's dream.

Growing up, Candace loved the game but was nervous about following in her family's basketball footsteps in case she didn't live up to the standards of their play. Her father encouraged her and began coaching Candace in eighth grade. He could see that, as well as her athletic ability, she had a vast knowledge of the game, so he challenged her to train hard and set her ambitions high.

Candace was soon on her very own winning path. At her high school, she set a record of 2,768 points and 1,592 rebounds in the 121 games she played. Throughout her three years at the University of Tennessee, Candace continued to excel and was the only college player to be selected for the US squad in the 2006 FIBA World Championships for Women.

Candace hit the pro scene in 2008, as the WNBA Draft's very first pick for the Los Angeles Sparks. In June that year, she became the second woman in WNBA history to land a dunk and then the first woman to dunk twice in one match. She went on to play for the national team at the 2008 Summer

Olympics, helping the team to secure eight victories and win gold.

After some time off to have her daughter and recover from an injury, Candace re-signed for the Sparks in 2012. She helped them score a 24–10 record in her first season back and, in the same year, helped Team USA defend their gold medal in the London Olympics.

She might be a forward at heart but Candace is well known for her all-round performance. She was crowned WNBA's Most Valuable Player (MVP) in her very first All-Star game in 2013 and was at the forefront of the Sparks' continuing success over the years. In 2016 she led them to win their first WNBA Finals championship since 2002. The same year, she was named in the WNBA's Top 20@20, a list celebrating the league's 20 best players for their twentieth anniversary.

Whether it's for scoring triple doubles or making history with her stat lines, Candace has earned her place in basketball history for so much more than some superb slam dunks. Off the court, Candace is raising her beautiful daughter, supporting charities close to her heart (such as the Pat Summitt Foundation and People for the Ethical Treatment of Animals) and working as a studio analyst for basketball tournament coverage. No rest for the basketball elite, hey…

HER AWESOME ACHIEVEMENTS

➔ The only player to have ever won the *USA Today* High School Player of the year award twice, scooping it in both 2003 and 2004.

➔ Crowned Gatorade's Female Basketball Player of the Year twice (2003 and 2004), Gatorade Female Athlete of the Year (2004) and McDonald's All-American (2004).

➔ The only person to win Rookie of the Year and MVP in WNBA in the same season (2008).

➔ Has played for various teams across the world including UMMC Ekaterinburg, Guangdong Dolphins and Xinjiang Tianshan Deers. But her main club was always the Sparks.

"MALE ATHLETES DON'T GET DROPPED WHEN THEY FATHER KIDS."

DANICA PATRICK

25 MARCH 1982–PRESENT

HER SUPERPOWERS:

It takes dedication and determination to shatter glass ceilings and break boundaries in the male-dominated motorsports world. Thankfully, Danica Patrick has both in engine-loads.

HER INCREDIBLE STORY

Danica Patrick is the most successful American woman in open-wheel racing – a motorsport in a highly modified, single-seated vehicle that has wheels outside its main body.

No stranger to racing non-traditional cars, Danica started karting at the age of ten, and not just for fun – she won the World Karting Association Grand National Championship three times before she was a teenager. But her early years weren't all trophies and smiles; Danica crashed into a concrete wall in one of her races due to a brake failure. Thankfully, she escaped without injury.

At 16, Danica dropped out of school in Wisconsin to move to the UK and follow her motorsports dream. It was no easy transition. Despite support from Formula One champions Jackie Stewart and Jenson Button, Danica faced judgement for being both female and American. This only made her more independent and determined. She took part in Formula Vauxhall and came second in the 2000 Formula Ford Festival before returning to the USA.

Danica made her debut in the IndyCar Series at Indianapolis 500 in 2005. She stunned viewers by leading in 19 laps and finishing in fourth place. She gained three pole positions in the series and was named Rookie of the Year. But Danica was just getting revved up. In 2008, she made motorsports history again when she became the first – and only

– woman to win an IndyCar Series, with her victory in the Indy Japan 300.

Her major-league success didn't happen overnight. Danica learned from every lap and race and continued to challenge herself and up her game. She soon turned her attention to higher spec stock cars and started competing in the NASCAR Cup Series in 2012, making headlines worldwide when she won a pole position for the fastest qualifying lap in the 2013 Daytona 500. She finished eighth in the race – the highest finishing position ever for a woman.

Until the day she retired, Danica continued to break records in the racing world. She achieved the most top 10 finishes by any woman in the NASCAR Cup Series and ended her career on a high with the "Danica Double", competing in both the Daytona 500 and the Indianapolis 500 in the same year (2018).

The tiny size of open-wheel cars and fast movements needed call for huge amounts of body strength and flexibility, so it's no surprise Danica turned her attention to health and fitness. Since retiring, she's launched a sportswear brand, published a fitness book and started a podcast.

HER AWESOME ACHIEVEMENTS

→ Competed in every NASCAR Cup Series race in 2013, becoming the first female driver to complete an entire season in the series.

→ Finished tenth in 2012 Xfinity Series points, earning the highest points finish by a woman in the history of NASCAR's top three series (Cup, Xfinity, Truck).

→ Named one of *TIME*'s "100 Most Influential People" in 2010.

→ The only person to have won the Monster Energy Fan Vote for the Monster Energy NASCAR All-Star Race more than once.

"GIVE YOURSELF PERMISSION TO SHOOT FOR SOMETHING THAT SEEMS TOTALLY BEYOND YOUR GRASP. YOU MAY BE SURPRISED AT YOUR CAPABILITIES."

DINA ASHER-SMITH

4 December 1995–Present

HER SUPERPOWERS:

Britain's fastest woman, Dina Asher-Smith puts the champ in champion. She's been breaking records and, quite literally, chasing her dreams since she was 13.

HER INCREDIBLE STORY

Being the fastest *ever* woman in British history is an incredible achievement, and most athletes can only dream of gaining that accolade before the age of 25.

Geraldina "Dina" Rachel Asher-Smith started breaking records early. She landed her first world record at just 13 years old, when she set the age-best time for the 300 m (39.16 seconds). It wasn't Dina's first victory, either. She'd been wowing onlookers and winning races since she joined the Blackheath and Bromley Harriers Athletic Club aged eight. It was there that she met her "second dad" and coach John Blackie, who's been coaching Dina and cheering her across the finish line ever since.

At just 17 years old, Dina won her first golds (yup, plural) when she stole the show at the European Junior Championships, winning the 200 m and 4 x 100-m relay (making her the youngest ever female World Championship relay medallist). A year later, she went worldwide, winning the 100 m at the 2014 World Junior Championships in 11.23 seconds. It was a pivotal year for Dina. On the bus to the European Athletic Championship heats, she found out she'd got the A Level results she needed to study history at King's College London. She described it as the best morning of her life.

Dina made her first senior sprinting debut while studying for her degree in 2015 – naturally she won, scooping the 60 m gold at the British Indoor Track and Field Championships. That summer, Dina reset history when she became the first British woman to run the 100 m in under 11 seconds.

In her 2016 Olympic debut, Dina placed fifth in the 200 m and bronze in the relay. Despite breaking her foot, she continued to compete across the world in 2017, and she graduated from King's College in the same year. In 2018, she famously won a historic triple gold when she came first place in the 100-m, 200-m and 4 x 100-m races at the European Championships in Berlin. She wrapped up the season as the world's fastest woman in the 200 m and joint fastest in the 100 m.

But what's her secret sauce for success? While training, body care and coaching are crucial, Dina believes "sprinting is a mental game". Before an event, Dina switches off from social media and distractions and focuses in on her practice. Her coach, John, reminds her to do her "normal" – not to dwell on others, or worry about not winning, but to focus on doing what she does best. And it's that self-focus that makes Dina one of the youngest, most "chilled" legends in the sporting world.

HER AWESOME ACHIEVEMENTS

→ Fastest woman in recorded British history, holding the record for both 100 m and 200 m in 2019.

→ Became first British woman in history to run 200 m in less than 22 seconds in 2018.

→ Named European Athlete of the Year by the European Athletics Organisation in 2018.

→ World's fastest teenage sprinter ever for distances over 60 m and 200 m.

"MY ADVICE? CAREFULLY CHOOSE WHOSE OPINION YOU VALUE AND TUNE OUT EVERYONE ELSE."

ELLEN MACARTHUR

8 JULY 1976–PRESENT

HER SUPERPOWERS:

Dame Ellen MacArthur single-handedly sailed around the world in 71 days not once but twice – and she's been making the world a more positive place ever since.

HER INCREDIBLE STORY

Sailing around the world is a once in a lifetime experience that very few people get to have – and it's a twice in a lifetime experience for even fewer. But Dame Ellen MacArthur managed to achieve this, and so much more, before the age of 30.

Ellen MacArthur is well known as one of the world's most successful solo long-distance yachtswomen. But rewind to her school days in Derbyshire, UK, and she was eating baked beans and mashed potatoes that cost 8p from the canteen, so she could save up the change to buy a boat. The first was an 8-ft dinghy named *Threp'ny Bit*. By the time she left school, she had three boats, which she sailed right up until she got her first sponsor.

Ellen's first circumnavigation was in 1995 when she sailed her dinner-money Corribee boat single-handed around Great Britain. She went on to her first solo transatlantic race a couple of years later, competing in a 21-ft Classe Mini yacht.

In 2001, Ellen attempted her first around-the-world competition in the non-stop Vendée Globe race. She finished in 94 days, 4 hours and 25 minutes, coming in in second place and sailing in a specially designed Kingfisher-sponsored yacht – quite the upgrade from her "dinner money boats"! It was a glass-ceiling-breaking moment for Ellen as she landed the world record for a single-handed, non-stop monohull circumnavigation by a woman and received a well-deserved MBE for her services to sport.

But what do you do after sailing around the world? Gear up to do it all over again, if you're Ellen MacArthur. After setting a new world record from Lower New York, USA, to Cornwall, UK, in 2004, Ellen turned her attentions back to circumnavigating the globe. She beat Frenchman Francis Joyon's world record for single-handedly sailing around the world in 2005 when she covered 27,354 nautical miles in 71 days, 14 hours, 18 minutes and 33 seconds.

Just a day after returning to England, Ellen was made a Dame and became the youngest ever recipient of the DBE (Dame Commander of the Most Excellent Order of the British Empire). She was also granted the rank of Honorary Lieutenant Commander the same day.

Ellen retired from sailing in 2009, deciding to switch her focus from circumnavigation to circular economy: a framework that aims to transform from the take-make-waste industrial model to regenerative natural systems and renewable energy products. The Ellen MacArthur Foundation encourages businesses and individuals to redesign the future with a focus on sustainability and positive change.

As if changing the world wasn't enough, this iconic sportswoman also fronts the Ellen MacArthur Cancer Trust. The charity takes young people aged 8–24 on sailing trips to help them rebuild confidence after cancer treatment and feel re-inspired for the future.

HER AWESOME ACHIEVEMENTS

→ World record holder for single-handed, non-stop, monohull circumnavigation by a woman with a time of 94 days, 4 hours and 25 minutes.

→ Record holder for single-handed monohull east-to-west passage by a woman, for sailing from Plymouth, UK, to Newport, USA, in 14 days, 23 hours and 11 minutes.

→ Appointed a Knight of the French Legion of Honour in March 2008.

→ Founded the Ellen MacArthur Foundation to promote a circular economy, after spending four years travelling and researching the challenges our current global economy faces.

"YOU JUST CONCENTRATE ON COMING OUT THE OTHER SIDE."

GEVA KATE MENTOR

17 September 1984–present

HER SUPERPOWERS:

Mentor by name, mentor by nature, Geva Kate Mentor was voted world's best netballer and uses her platform to inspire others.

HER INCREDIBLE STORY

All too often, goalkeepers don't get the appreciation they deserve. But since being chosen for the England netball team at just 16, and playing her first Commonwealth Games in 2002, this 1.96-m Bournemouth-born sports star has gained over 300 caps and earned a reputation as one of the best defenders in the world. She's made history, broken records and saved hundreds of goals across the globe. But it hasn't always been international success and a bed of English Roses for Geva Mentor.

In 2008, Geva was playing for the Surrey Storm team earning £15 a match in between World Championships and Commonwealth Games. She became known for her perfect timing, positive outlook, great organization and stellar understanding of the game. Her commitment paid off and she started to receive worldwide recognition. Geva signed to play with the Adelaide Thunderbirds in the ANZ Championships in 2008 and she's been helping teams across the world win ever since.

Over the years, she's played in the ANZ Championships, winning titles with the Adelaide Thunderbirds (2010) and Melbourne Vixens (2014). In 2017, she also captained Sunshine Coast Lightning in the famous Suncorp Super Netball Premiership and was crowned World's Best Netballer. Well-deserved achievements for a world-class talent.

Australia might be her home from home but the England Roses will always have a special place in Geva's heart. In 2017, Geva shared her dream of winning gold with England in an interview. It came true just a year later. With Geva as goalkeeper, the England Roses achieved the best netball result in England's history when they won gold against Australia in the 2018 Commonwealth Games. The game was close but Geva's diligent defence held off the threat of Australia and helped her team come back from four points down in the final quarter.

After the unforgettable Commonwealth win, Geva headed back Down Under to help lead the defence for Melbourne's Collingwood Magpies. In her first season alone, aged 35, she totted up the second most defensive rebounds (33) and deflections (86) of all goal defenders in the league. She also won the Best, Fairest and Player's Player awards. All in a season's work for this superwoman!

When she's not storming the netball pitch, Geva puts her decades of wisdom to inspirational use by helping new players find balance between their personal life and netball career. It's something she has first-hand experience with, having gone through a divorce during the Commonwealth Games, and she speaks openly about freezing her eggs. As well as training 7.30 a.m. until 3 p.m. all week, she's also training to become a primary school teacher. You go, Geva.

HER AWESOME ACHIEVEMENTS

→ Played five Commonwealth Games for the England Roses: 2002, 2006, 2010, 2014, 2018.

→ Over 140 England caps and over 160 caps in Australian championships.

→ Voted World's Best Netballer in 2014 and 2017 (*The Guardian*).

→ Received a CBE for her services to netball in 2019.

"LISTEN TO ADVICE, BUT REMEMBER TO STAY TRUE TO YOURSELF."

IBTIHAJ MUHAMMAD

4 DECEMBER 1985–PRESENT

HER SUPERPOWERS:

Proud Muslim, game-changing Olympian and the first US woman to fence in a hijab, it's the incredible Ibtihaj Muhammad.

HER INCREDIBLE STORY

It was a defining moment for the Olympics when, in 2016, Ibtihaj Muhammad walked out for her fencing event, proudly wearing a hijab. Right there in Rio, she became the first US woman to compete in the Olympics wearing a hijab *and* the first Muslim-American woman to win an Olympic medal.

Ibtihaj's whole life had led up to that moment. She'd loved sports from a young age, but her parents found that sporting attire often conflicted with their religious beliefs about dressing modestly. Many times, Ibtihaj's mum would sew longer sleeves onto tops or cover her daughter's legs. So, when they spotted the fencing team practising one night, her mum looked at their trousers and hats and thought "perfect".

Ibtihaj joined her school fencing team aged 13 and originally started training with an épée fencing sword, but it wasn't long before her coach had her switch to a sabre – considered the fastest and most powerful sword. She excelled from there and, in 2002, Ibtihaj joined the Peter Westbrook Foundation, a non-profit organization that teaches underprivileged young people to fence. She went on to be crowned captain of her high school fencing team and the 2005 Junior Olympic Champion, before joining the US national fencing team in 2010.

After more than a decade of practice, the 2016 Rio Olympics was a huge deal – not just for Ibtihaj, but also for her family and the Muslim community. She won her first duel, and while she missed out on victory in her second, she certainly made history. Ibtihaj took home an Olympic bronze medal in fencing and won the hearts of millions of people across the world.

Ibtihaj is as fierce an activist as she is a fencer. Never one to sit on the fence (sorry!), she has travelled the world speaking out about equality and breaking down barriers to empower girls through sport and education.

Ibtihaj has faced many struggles due to the lack of suitable hijabs available for sports professionals. She frequently received warnings in games due to being unable to hear referees' instructions, because the material of her hijab would become stiff when it came into contact with any sweat. It also didn't fit well with her fencing uniform; Ibtihaj had to tuck extra fabric into her sports bra straps so it would stay put. She became one of the first models and ambassadors to sport the Nike Pro performance hijab, made of light, soft, flexible and breathable fabric.

While Ibtihaj may have been the first US female Olympian to wear a hijab, something tells me she won't be the last.

HER AWESOME ACHIEVEMENTS

→ Became the first Muslim-American woman to win an Olympic medal and compete wearing a hijab in 2016.

→ Named Muslim Sportswoman of the Year in 2012.

→ Five-time Senior World medalist and World Champion.

→ Serves as an ambassador on the US Department of State's Empowering Women and Girls Through Sport initiative.

"I OWE IT TO PEOPLE WHO LOOK LIKE ME. THESE STRUGGLES, THIS EVERYDAY FEARMONGERING AND HATE THAT WE ARE EXPERIENCING — I OWE IT TO ALL OF US TO COMBAT THESE THINGS. I HAVE TO SPEAK OUT AGAINST IT BECAUSE THERE WERE PEOPLE BEFORE ME THAT DID."

JEAN DRISCOLL

18 November 1966–present

HER SUPERPOWERS:

From bed-bound and feeling hopeless to breaking records at the Boston Marathon and Paralympic Games, Jean Driscoll is a pioneer like no other.

HER INCREDIBLE STORY

Today, she's in the US Olympic Hall of Fame for her epic achievements. But being a sporting superstar was never something Jean Driscoll imagined as a child.

Jean was born with spina bifida, a condition where the spine doesn't develop fully in the womb. This left her unable to walk with ease and made childhood especially tough. As she didn't have a wheelchair in her early years, Jean's siblings would pull her to and from school in a wagon.

Aged 13, Jean fell off her bike and had to have five major hip operations. She went from wearing foot braces to a whole body cast for a year. The only thing that got her through was the slight hope she'd be able to walk better than before when the cast came off. But that wasn't the case. The damage was irreparable and Jean became a wheelchair user, leaving her feeling "suicidal" and like "a burden".

It was in her lowest moment that a friend invited her to a wheelchair soccer game. She was initially nervous about it being an "adapted" game but her preconceptions changed the moment she arrived. Chairs were crashing, bodies were ducking and diving — the atmosphere was electric. There and then, she found a whole new love of sport.

Sports soon became Jean's hope. She was scouted by a wheelchair basketball recruiter at college and, in a matter of years, went from being bed-bound and feeling lost to becoming one of the most impressive sporting champions around. In her first year at the University of Illinois, she excelled at wheelchair basketball and track and field. In 1988, she competed in her first Paralympics, taking home gold in the 4 x 200-m relay, silver in the 100-m relay and bronze in the 200-m and 400-m races.

After winning in a 12-km wheelchair race in 1989, Jean's coach suggested she try for a marathon. At first, she wasn't sure, thinking 26.2 miles was too far, but, in true Jean style, she gave it a go anyway. She did so well in her first wheelchair marathon (the Chicago Marathon in 1989) that she qualified for the 1990 Boston Marathon. And after six months of gruelling training, she won the women's wheelchair division. In fact, she broke her category's record by seven seconds and began her seven-year winning streak.

Jean continued to compete in the Paralympics between marathons and won four more golds, two silvers and two bronzes. She claimed her eighth and final Boston Marathon victory in 2000, giving her the incredible record of more wins than any other Boston marathoner.

Jean's story is a lesson in not giving up, despite the cards that life deals you. And it's a story that has seen her earn her rightful place in sporting history.

HER AWESOME ACHIEVEMENTS

➜ Inducted into the US Olympic Hall of Fame in 2012.

➜ Granted the Order of Lincoln award from The Lincoln Academy of Illinois, the highest honour of the State of Illinois, in 2012.

➜ Motivational speaker and philanthropist for athletes with disabilities.

➜ Travelled to Ghana to support programmes to help coach the country's first Paralympic athletes.

"I BELIEVE THE BIGGEST LIMITS ARE THE ONES WE PLACE ON OURSELVES OR ALLOW OTHERS TO PLACE ON US."

JESSICA ENNIS-HILL

28 JANUARY 1986–PRESENT

HER SUPERPOWERS:

From strength to strength and setback to comeback, Dame Jessica Ennis-Hill is an Olympic legend who's shown unflinching tenacity at every step of her career.

HER INCREDIBLE STORY

Long jump, high jump, hurdles, shotput, javelin, 200 m and 800 m – they're all challenging athletic events in their own right, but combine them together and it's no surprise that heptathlon is one of the hardest track and field events of all time. Over the last decades, Jessica Ennis-Hill has taken the event in her impressive stride, becoming one of the most decorated heptathletes in the world.

Sport was a big part of Jessica's life from an early age. At just ten years old, she went along to a local athletics event in her home city of Sheffield, UK. She won a pair of trainers there and met her longstanding coach, Toni Minichiello. The rest, as they say, is history.

Jessica's first senior victory came aged 18, when she won the 2004 Northern Senior Indoor Championships 60-m hurdles in just 8.60 seconds. She then broke the British under-23 heptathlon record in 2007, jumping 1.95 m and winning with 6,388 points in Desenzano. The same year, she set two lifetime bests at javelin and 800 m.

Jessica's successful career wasn't without setbacks. In 2008, she endured stress fractures in her right foot and had to pull out of the Beijing Olympics. She trained hard, rebuilt strength in her foot and made one heck of a comeback in 2009. Jessica landed a record-breaking win at the World Combined Events in Desenzano, despite having to change her take-off leg for the long jump from right to left. She then won gold, and set a new personal best of 6,731 points, at the 2009 Berlin World Championships – it was the highest heptathlon score that year.

Jessica finally took home her Olympic gold in the 2012 London Games. She won first place in the heptathlon and grounded her all-time personal best of 6,955. It was an iconic event for Jessica. At the end of her first day, she'd landed her highest ever scores, two personal bests *and* set a new British record for the fastest time ever run in a heptathlon. She was recognized as the *Sunday Times*' Sportswoman of the Year and given a CBE in the same year.

After taking some time out to marry her childhood sweetheart and give birth to baby Reggie, Jessica retired on a high – having made a winning comeback in the 2015 World Championships and scooped silver at the 2016 Rio Olympics. Today, when she's not campaigning for charities, looking after her two children or being a remarkable role model, she's writing children's books. Goals.

HER AWESOME ACHIEVEMENTS

➜ Upgraded from MBE to OBE to DBE (Damehood) for her services to athletics.

➜ Seven-time gold champion, landing the top podium spot at the 2012 Olympics, the World Championships (2009, 2011 and 2015), World Indoor Championships (2010), European Championships (2010) and European Junior Championships (2005).

➜ First British woman to win BBC Sports Personality of the Year Lifetime Achievement Award in 2017.

➜ Previously held British records in the 100-m hurdles, high jump and heptathlon.

"I'M PROUD OF THE WAY I'VE DEALT WITH SETBACKS. IT'S HARD WHEN YOU FEEL DOWN AND YOU THINK, 'WHY IS THE WORLD DOING THIS TO ME?' BUT YOU HAVE TO PICK YOURSELF UP AGAIN. THAT'S WHAT MAKES YOU A BETTER ATHLETE."

KATHLEEN "KATIE" GENEVIEVE LEDECKY

17 MARCH 1997–PRESENT

HER SUPERPOWERS:

Superstar swimmer, Olympic gold winner, record breaker – and all before the age of 25. Go, Katie Ledecky!

HER INCREDIBLE STORY

"I just like to swim fast. I don't think about distance." It's a simple motto but one that's seen Katie Ledecky swim her way to five Olympic and 15 World Championship golds.

Born in 1997 in Washington, DC, Katie started swimming at six, and by the time she left school she'd set national junior records and was the record holder in every swimming race except the 100-m breaststroke at her school.

She took on her first Olympics in 2012, at just 15 years old. It was her very first senior national competition and came as a moment that stunned the world. Having placed third in the heats, the newcomer swam faster than the legends alongside her in the 800-m freestyle and won gold with a time of 8:14:63.

The Olympics were just the start of Katie's history-making. In the 2013 World Championships, she won golds in the 400 m, 800 m, 1,500-m freestyle, and in the 4 x 200-m freestyle. She also set two new world records, slicing six seconds off the 1,500-m record and beating Rebecca Adlington's world record in the 800-m freestyle with a time of 8:13.86. In both events, Katie let other swimmers lead for most of the race before moving in and stealing the show in the last few hundred metres.

Katie won five more golds and broke two more records (400 m and 1,500 m) in the 2014 Pan Pacific

Championships. She then maintained her epic trend of five golds in the 2015 World Championships and broke not one, not two, but three world records. This saw Katie become the first ever swimmer to win the 200 m, 400 m, 800 m, 1,500 m and 4 x 200-m freestyle in a major championship.

In her second Olympic Games, Rio 2016, Katie set an Olympic record in the heats when she qualified for the 400 m with a legendary time of 3:58.71. She won the race itself with a world record of 3:56.41. She also took home gold in the 200 m and set a new world record in the 800 m, winning with a game-changing time of 8:04.79. Her individual successes were stellar, but her relay performance was sensational. Taking the last 200-m lap in the 4 x 200-m freestyle, Katie took the team from being 0.89 seconds behind to a golden 1.84 seconds ahead. It was an epic show that saw Katie become the first female swimmer to win the 200 m, 400 m and 800 m since 1968, earning her place as the year's most decorated female Olympian.

Katie continues to snatch gold at championships, while making time to inspire a generation of female swimmers and win countless awards.

HER AWESOME ACHIEVEMENTS

→ *Swimming World* World Swimmer of the Year for five years (2013, 2014, 2015, 2016, 2018).

→ Youngest person on the *Time 100* list in 2016.

→ Voted top swimmer of the decade, ahead of Michael Phelps, by *SwimSwam.com* readers and International Sportswoman of the Decade by *London Evening Standard* voters.

→ The most decorated female swimming champion in history, with five Olympic gold medals and 15 World Championship gold medals.

"SET GOALS THAT, WHEN YOU SET THEM, YOU THINK THEY'RE IMPOSSIBLE. BUT THEN EVERY DAY YOU CAN WORK TOWARDS THEM, AND ANYTHING IS POSSIBLE, SO KEEP WORKING HARD AND FOLLOW YOUR DREAMS."

KERRI WALSH JENNINGS AND MISTY MAY-TREANOR

15 August 1978–present and
30 July 1977–present

THEIR SUPERPOWERS:

*The American duo who ruled the sand for over a decade.
Say hello to the Queen and Queen of volleyball.*

THEIR INCREDIBLE STORY

Volleyball is about so much more than bikinis and beautiful beaches. It's about trust, togetherness and teamwork – and Kerri and Misty are testament to all three.

The pair met as sporty teenagers on the high school indoor volleyball scene. They admired each other's skills from a distance for years, before their ambition brought them back together in 2001. By the end of 2001, the duo were ranking fifth in the world, and in 2002, they'd made it to number one.

They won an incredible 90 consecutive matches in 2003 and entered their first Olympics in 2004 with one goal only: to bring home gold. In the semi-finals, they beat Misty's previous partner, Holly McPeak, and Elaine Young, and went on to defeat Brazil in the finals. They left Athens clutching their gold, as the first American female duo to win Olympic gold in beach volleyball.

The duo dominated beach volleyball for over a decade, breaking records, racking up winning streaks and becoming the sport's female force to be reckoned with.

After repeating the May-Treanor–Walsh winning magic at the 2008 Beijing Olympics, it was the start of a short hiatus for the legendary duo. Misty went on to star on *Dancing with the Stars* in 2009 but had to stop after she injured her Achilles tendon and needed surgery. Meanwhile, Kerri gave birth to two beautiful children. With so much going on in their lives off court, it was hit-and-miss as to whether they'd compete in the 2012 Olympics.

But they weren't quite done. The duo took their spot on the sand in London 2012 and went down in history with their third consecutive Olympic gold win. "The first two gold medals were about volleyball," Misty said. "This was so much more about the friendship, the togetherness, the journey." Leaving on a high, Misty retired from the game shortly after, drawing a decade of spectacular success to a close.

Three Olympic wins, one incredible impact, but what's their secret? Trust and partnership. Teamwork really did make Kerri and Misty's dream work. The pair had different sporting personalities – Kerri was bold and boisterous with a famous block while Misty was quietly confident with awesome jumping abilities – but they complemented each other perfectly. They'd practise storm or shower, both on and off the pitch. Giving up was never an option. And while their volleyball partnership is over, their friendship is as strong as ever.

THEIR AWESOME ACHIEVEMENTS

→ Competed in 77 FIVB (Fédération Internationale de Volleyball) tournaments between 2001 and 2012, winning 40, coming second 14 times and third six times.

→ Winners of five AVP (Association of Volleyball Professionals) Team of the Year awards (2003–2007).

→ Triple Olympic gold winners for beach volleyball (2004, 2008, 2012).

→ During their Olympic matches from 2004 to 2012, they won all 21 matches and lost only one set (in 2012).

→ Won an incredible 112 championship matches in a row across domestic and international competitions.

"DON'T GET DISCOURAGED; THERE ARE GOING TO BE EBBS AND FLOWS." – MISTY MAY-TREANOR

"BREATHE, BELIEVE, BATTLE." – KERRI WALSH JENNINGS

ALEXIS NOEL "LEXI" THOMPSON

10 FEBRUARY 1995–PRESENT

HER SUPERPOWERS:

From qualifying for the US Women's Open at 12 to winning the LPGA (Ladies Professional Golf Association) tournament at 16, Lexi Thompson's career has swung from success to success from a young age.

HER INCREDIBLE STORY

The average age of a US Golf Open champion is 32. Lexi Thompson defied all age barriers when she qualified for the US Women's Open at just 12 years old. It was a fairly natural progression for her, given that she'd already won the US Kids Golf World Championship twice and had two professional golfer brothers.

Lexi grew up on the golf course in Coral Springs, Florida, and earned her first hole-in-one at just seven years old. She was so passionate about golf, in fact, that she started being home schooled in 12th grade so she could spend more time on the course.

Lexi missed the cut in the US Women's Open tournaments by a matter of strokes in 2007 and 2008, and finished 34th in the 2009 competition. But even at such a young age, giving up wasn't in her nature. She practised and perfected her technique and, in 2010, she finished 12 strokes behind the winner in the Women's Australian Open and went undefeated in the Curtis Cup. It was just the boost she needed. Lexi turned pro in June 2010, aged 15. Her first professional tournament was at the 2010 US Women's Open, where she finished tenth at the prestigious Oakmount County Club.

In 2011, Lexi made a memorable petition to the Ladies Professional Golf Association to allow her to play in the tournament at 16 years old. Her membership was granted and she made an incredible debut, winning the Navistar Classic competition and becoming the youngest winner.

As well as taking home gold at the Dubai Ladies Masters on the Ladies European Tour (LET), with a four-stroke margin in 2011, Lexi won numerous LPGA competitions between 2013 and 2017. In 2014, she landed her first major championship win at the Kraft Nabisco Championship and became the second youngest LPGA golfer to win a major at 19. She celebrated her victory by jumping into Poppie's Pond at the Mission Hills Country Club in California.

From LPGAs to ANZs and Indy tournaments, Lexi's a consistent winner. But her time on and off the course hasn't been without its struggles. In 2018, she pulled out of the Ricoh Women's British Open and announced that she was taking some time to "recharge her mental batteries" and focus on life outside of golf. Her mum had recently been diagnosed with cancer and she bravely opened up about her own struggles "mentally and emotionally". In true Lexi style, she came back with her best ever performance, tying second in the US Women's Open in 2019. She remains a role model when it comes to balancing work, life, emotions and struggles.

HER AWESOME ACHIEVEMENTS

➜ Aged 12, Lexi set the record for the youngest person to ever qualify for the US Women's Open in 2007.

➜ Ranks in the top five youngest LPGA major winners.

➜ Ranked in the top five Women's World Golfing Rankings between 2015 and 2018.

➜ Had her best season's earnings, totalling $1,793,904, for her efforts in 2015–2016.

"YOU GO THROUGH SLUMPS IN THIS GAME, AND YOU JUST HAVE TO WORK THROUGH THEM. YOU'RE GOING TO MISS PUTTS... AND HAVE BAD ROUNDS. YOU JUST HAVE TO THINK TO YOURSELF THAT YOU ALWAYS HAVE TOMORROW."

LINDSEY CAROLINE VONN

18 October 1984–present

HER SUPERPOWERS:

She made her World Cup debut downhill skiing at just 16 and quickly became one of the greatest skiers the world has ever seen. All hail Lindsey V.

HER INCREDIBLE STORY

Reaching speeds of 130 kmph in a car can be daunting, let alone hitting that speed on skis. For Lindsey Vonn, it's more than just a thrill – it's a passion.

Lindsey learned to ski at just two years old. Her beloved grandfather would teach her on family vacations. By the time she was seven, she'd skied in Minnesota, Colorado and Oregon and was a member of Erich Sailer's ski development programme.

At nine, she crossed paths with her skiing idol, Picabo Street. It was the moment she knew she wanted to "become a ski racer". Picabo trained Lindsey some years later and described her talent as "the best".

Like most sporting success stories, Lindsey's wasn't without its lows. She found herself wanting to quit in 2000 when she crashed in 50 out of 55 races. "I kept falling and couldn't figure out how not to fall. But I made a decision that I'd keep going."

Keep going, she did. That same year, Lindsey trained hard, got better and better, and her World Cup debut arrived. She then competed in the 2002 Winter Olympics, finishing sixth, before taking home medals in both the 2003 Fédération Internationale de Ski and 2004 US Alpine Championships.

Lindsey's career nearly came crashing down when she crashed during training for the 2006 Winter Olympics and had to be airlifted to hospital.

Unbelievably, she returned to compete in the same event and was presented with the US Olympic Spirit Award.

In her 2008 comeback, Lindsey won the women's World Cup overall title and set a new American record for ten World Cup downhill race victories. She then landed her first Olympic gold in the 2010 Winter Olympics. She went on to dominate the World Cup across downhill, super-G, combined and slalom, making her one of only six women to have won World Cup races in all disciplines of alpine skiing.

After a hiatus due to injury, Lindsey headed back to the slopes in 2017 and won a bronze in the downhill race at the World Championships. This saw her become the oldest woman to win a medal in the event's history, aged 32 and fabulous. In true Lindsey style, she kept going and won another bronze at the 2018 Winter Olympics.

Lindsey reluctantly retired in 2019 due to continued injury. Having had her eyes on another Olympic gold, she said it was the hardest decision of her life. However, 82 World Cup wins, four overall World Cup titles, three Olympic medals and eight World Championship medals is an outstanding achievement and one that will see Lindsey forever recognized as one of the most successful skiers in history.

HER AWESOME ACHIEVEMENTS

➜ An amazing total of 82 international victories in 14 years.

➜ Ranked number one greatest female alpine skier of all time in the FIS Alpine Ski World Cup rankings.

➜ Won both the prestigious Laureus Sportswoman of the Year award and the United States Olympic Committee's sportswoman of the year award in 2010.

"THE RUSH OF SKIING 80-PLUS MILES PER HOUR DOWN A MOUNTAIN JUST NEVER GETS OLD."

MAGGIE ALPHONSI

20 December 1983–present

HER SUPERPOWERS:

*Born with a club foot, Maggie Alphonsi defied all odds
to take women's rugby to new heights and become one
of the most successful players of all time.*

HER INCREDIBLE STORY

She's known as "the face of international women's rugby" and has represented England a whopping 74 times. But Maggie Alphonsi's path to rugby wasn't quite the traditional one you might imagine.

Born on a football-obsessed council estate in Lewisham, London, her first ever job was wrapping burgers in McDonalds. Maggie found herself prioritizing socializing over studying as a teenager, which resulted in her spending a lot of time in the headmistress's office.

A chat with a PE teacher first sparked her interest in rugby. When the teacher first suggested it, Maggie shrugged it off for three reasons: she was a girl, she was black and she walked with a limp due to her club foot. She'd never seen anyone like her on the rugby pitch or playing any high-level sport, for that matter. But with a bit of persuasion, Maggie went to the Saracens club, asking to train. She surprised herself by how good she was and for the first time in Maggie's life, she felt free, like "neither gender nor ethnic origin mattered". It was the start of something special.

Maggie progressed quickly at Saracens and took to fundraising outside school to make the £2,000 needed to get to Australia for try-outs. At 18, she was chosen for the England Academy squad and won her first Test cap a year later.

She made her England Rugby debut in 2003 as flanker, running and tackling with incredible power and speed. In her following pro years, Maggie played two World Cups, helped the England team win the Six Nations a record seven times in a row, scored 28 tries and earned 74 caps.

It's safe to say she has defied stereotypes, kicking women's rugby up on the sporting agenda. When she started out, Maggie would have to change in the toilets – because men were given the changing rooms – and wear men's hand-me-downs because "no one wanted to buy brand new strips for women's teams". Things aren't perfect now but they've changed significantly – and a lot of that is down to Maggie's influence.

Maggie retired on a high, after leading the England Women's team to their game-changing 2014 World Cup victory. It was the first time they'd won in 20 years. Post-retirement, she coaches, mentors and serves on the rugby union council, leading diversity and inclusion agendas. She does it all to break boundaries and inspire young women to take up the sport. "In ten years' time, I really hope women are in leadership roles across all sports," Maggie has said. Her career on the pitch may be done but her legacy definitely lives strong.

HER AWESOME ACHIEVEMENTS

→ Awarded an MBE for her services to the rugby union.

→ Was the first ever female winner of the Pat Marshall award from the Rugby Union Writers' Club.

→ Became the first female rugby pundit to cover a men's championship rugby match in 2015.

→ Became the first England Women's player to be elected as a National Member of the Rugby Football Union's Council in 2016 and has a leading role on the Diversity and Inclusion steering group.

"LIFE IS MEASURED BY THE IMPACT YOU HAVE ON OTHER PEOPLE. IT'S ABOUT WHO YOU WANT TO INSPIRE, WHO YOU CAN BE A ROLE MODEL FOR. SO, YOU HAVE TO ASK YOURSELF, 'WHAT CAN YOU DO TO INSPIRE OTHERS?'"

MARIE-PHILIP POULIN

28 MARCH 1991–PRESENT

HER SUPERPOWERS:

The ice hockey player who scored the winning two goals in an Olympic final, Marie-Philip is a puck-whizzing extraordinaire.

HER INCREDIBLE STORY

With two Olympic golds and a silver medal under her ice hockey belt, plus countless awards and success in eight world championships, it's little surprise that Marie-Philip Poulin is praised as being one of the best female ice hockey players in the world.

Marie was no stranger to the ice from an early age. She started figure skating at four years old but soon decided it wasn't for her and moved to ice hockey. When she saw the Canadian women's team play against the USA at the Olympics aged ten, she knew that was where she wanted to be.

Fast forward to 2010 and Marie was skating onto the scene for her first Olympic Games on home ice in Vancouver. At 18, she was the youngest player on Canada's team – but that didn't hold her back. She scored five goals and two assists in total, playing her signature position of forward. And in a nail-biting final game, Marie-Philip drove the only two goals of the match into the net.

The next time Marie-Philip headed to the Olympics in 2014, she was well-established as a star player, but no one could have predicted just how greatly she'd perform. In a tense final, the Canadian team found themselves 2–1 down to the USA with just 54.6 seconds left on the clock. Marie-Philip spotted an opportunity and darted to secure the tying goal. She then defied all odds in overtime, sliding the puck into the net and earning the team their second Olympic gold in an incredible turn of events.

Marie-Philip's reputation as a caring, supportive team player shone through when she led the team as captain in the Pyeongchang 2018 Winter Olympics. She played another epic show, driving the team 2–1 up, but they narrowly lost to the USA on shootouts. The event saw her become the only player in women's ice hockey to score in three consecutive Olympic finals.

The Olympics aren't the only championships Marie-Philip's excelled in. She's been a leading player in the Canadian Women's Hockey League (CWHL) and the International Ice Hockey Federation (IIHF). Following a CWHL stint as a "rookie", she re-joined in 2015, playing for Les Canadiennes de Montréal. She racked up 23 goals and 23 assists in that season alone. Her overall CWHL career goals sit at 100+ and she's been crowned MVP three times. She's also achieved seven silver team medals in the IIHF.

From playing against boys up until she was 15 to being dubbed one of the best female ice hockey players in the world, Marie-Philip has been on an incredible journey. She's inspired a generation, catapulted the popularity of the game forward – and she's just getting warmed up.

HER AWESOME ACHIEVEMENTS

→ The first and currently only female hockey player to score in three consecutive Olympic finals.

→ Earned a place in the Media All-Star Team after her performance in the 2010 Vancouver Olympics.

→ Awarded the prestigious Angela James Bowl three times.

"I HOPE I WILL BE REMEMBERED FOR THE HARD WORK, THE DEDICATION AND HOW I ALWAYS WANTED TO MAKE OTHERS BETTER. AND HOW MUCH FUN I HAD WHEN I WAS PLAYING."

MARTA VIEIRA DA SILVA

19 February 1986–PRESENT

HER SUPERPOWERS:

She's been compared to Pelé and has achieved things that no other footballer has – it's the one and only Marta Vieira da Silva.

HER INCREDIBLE STORY

Growing up in a small town in Brazil, Marta wasn't allowed to play football. Until 1981, it was illegal for women to play and it was still frowned upon when Marta was young. So she got creative. A shoeless young Marta would play with abandoned footballs and makeshift balls made of bundled grocery bags.

Her natural talent didn't go unnoticed and she eventually joined a local boys' junior team. The boys were desperate to win against her but Marta was swifter, more flexible and more creative in her approach from years of playing alone. She knew how to control the ball like no other.

At 14, Marta was scouted by a coach looking to start a women's team and soon started playing professionally. She spent some time playing for Santa Cruz, before joining Umeå IK in Sweden in 2004. Marta scored an amazing 22 league goals for Umeå and played in the 2004 UEFA Women's Cup final. In just three seasons with the team, she stacked up a total of 111 goals in 103 league games. She moved on for a brief stint at Los Angeles Sol, where she was voted MVP, before joining FC Gold Pride, California, in 2010. She helped them win two titles.

Marta changed the game of women's football in Brazil when she joined the Brazilian women's national team. She made her FIFA Women's World Cup debut in 2007, scoring three goals.

She then returned in 2007 for a spectacular show. Marta scored four goals in group stage, helping the team sail through to the quarter finals, where her penalty led to a 3–2 win against Australia. In the semi-finals, she scored two jaw-dropping goals in a match against the USA, who were favourites to win. Her second goal came in the 97th minute. Marta received the ball outside the box and soared it into the air and over a defender's shoulder with a single tap. She then dodged defence to land the ball in the back of the net. It was a 4–0 landslide win.

Marta received the overall "Golden Ball" for top individual player and the "Golden Boot" for top scorer with seven goals. She has continued to wow in World Cups since, achieving top spot for most goals scored (17) and becoming the only player – male or female – to score in five consecutive world cups.

There are a lot of reasons to celebrate Marta. She helped inspire a generation of epic female players in a time when football was seen as "a man's sport". In recognition of her work, she was announced as the UN Goodwill Ambassador for women and girls in sport in 2018.

HER AWESOME ACHIEVEMENTS

➔ Scored over 100 goals for Brazil since she started playing for them in 2002.

➔ Played a big part in the Brazilian national team that won silver medals at both the 2004 and 2008 Summer Olympics.

➔ Named FIFA World Player of the Year six times – from 2006 to 2010.

➔ Captained Brazil to their Copa América win in 2018.

"MY MESSAGE TO GIRLS EVERYWHERE IN THIS WORLD: BELIEVE IN YOURSELF AND TRUST YOURSELF, BECAUSE IF YOU DON'T BELIEVE IN YOURSELF, NO ONE ELSE WILL."

MAYA MOORE

11 JUNE 1989–PRESENT

HER SUPERPOWERS:

*Maya Moore's a winner. She's been slam dunkin'
championships since she leaped onto the basketball
scene at high school and has well and truly earned her
place in basketball history.*

HER INCREDIBLE STORY

Olympic golds, world championships, All-American awards – Maya Moore is no stranger to slam dunk success. Her love of the game began aged three, when her mum mounted a basketball hoop on the back of her bedroom door to keep her occupied while dinner was cooking. By the time she'd left high school, Maya had won three state titles, been voted National Gatorade Player of the Year and achieved epic stats of 2,664 points, 1,212 rebounds, 407 assists and 467 steals – all while managing to maintain a 4.0 grade average. At college she went on to win back-to-back national championships (2009 and 2010), leading the team as captain and setting the NCAA record by helping her team win 90 games in a row.

Her pro career started out with all the greatness of her high school and college record. In 2011, she became the first female to sign for Air Jordan and was drafted first overall by the Minnesota Lynx. Maya helped lead the team to their best record in history, winning five out of the six championships she played. She quickly went from star rookie to MVP and, in 2011, became only the second player in WNBA history to win Rookie of the Year and the WNBA championship in the same year.

Representing her country, Maya became the youngest member of the gold-winning US Olympic team in 2012. It was the beginning of her Olympic success and Maya helped lead the team to another golden victory in Rio in 2016.

Her basketball career has taken her right across the globe. Maya has won both the EuroLeague and Spanish league titles. She also led China's Shanxi Flame to their first ever WBCA championship, snatching the title for three years running between 2013 and 2015. It's little wonder that she's established a place as one of the greatest basketball players in history. As well as her four WNBA championship wins, Moore achieved Most Valuable Player of the FIBA World Championships after leading Shanxi to its ninth gold medal in 2014. She's also the first pro athlete (male or female) to stack up three titles – Rookie of the Year, All-Star MVP and League MVP – in just five seasons of play.

In early 2020, Maya took a sabbatical from basketball to dedicate her time to fighting for criminal justice reform – just one of many ways she uses her platform for positive change.

HER AWESOME ACHIEVEMENTS

➜ Two-time Olympic gold winner (2012 and 2016) and six time WNBA All-Star winner (2011, 2013–2015, 2017 and 2018).

➜ Impeccable stateside win-lose rate of 497–78.

➜ Named the "greatest female basketball player in history" when crowned as Performer of the Year by *Sports Illustrated* in 2017.

➜ Invited to honours sessions at the White House five times, leading to Obama joking that "basically, there's like a Maya Moore wing in the White House".

"EVERY TIME YOU PLAY ANYTHING, THERE'S A CHANCE THAT YOU CAN WIN. THERE'S NO REASON NOT TO COMPETE NO MATTER WHAT YOU'RE PLAYING."

MEGAN ANNA RAPINOE

5 JULY 1985–PRESENT

HER SUPERPOWERS:

Pink hair, do care. Megan Rapinoe is much more than just a world-renowned soccer player; she's a true game-changer who exemplifies the term "activist".

HER INCREDIBLE STORY

One stealthy left kick for America, one big step for womankind. When Megan Rapinoe scored her 61st-minute goal in the 2019 FIFA Women's World Cup Final, it was more than just some winning footwork for the country. It was symbolic of the game-changing trajectory that women's football was on – a sign that women's football was here to stay and deserved some long overdue respect, equality and fairness.

Gender equality isn't just a talking point for Megan. In the same year as her stellar World Cup performance, Megan joined forces with 28 other female football champions to file a lawsuit against the United States Soccer Federation, demanding equal pay. The lawsuit called out the fact that male players got paid around $30,000 more (plus bonuses) for wins and over two times more than women's teams for World Cups. For many years, it had gone under the radar, but not on Megan's watch. "We show up for a game, if we win the game, if we lose the game, if we tie the game, we want to be paid equally, period."

Megan spent her youth being coached, along with her twin sister, Rachael, by her dad. For both of them, soccer was a good way of escaping the drug abuse problem that was rife in rural California when they were growing up. Megan played for Elk Grove Pride in the Woman's Premier Soccer League, along with her sister and fellow national team player Stephanie Cox. She was voted the winner of the prestigious "All-American" award as both a junior and senior. After high school, both Megan and her twin attended the University of Portland. Playing for the All-West Coast Conference, Megan started all 25 games midfield, scored 15 goals and assisted 13.

From America to Australia and France to FIFA, Megan has played for a variety of teams and leagues, but two things have always been consistent: her performance and her fight for equality. She's worked her magic in three FIFA World Cups (2011, 2015 and 2019) and one Olympic Games (2012), scoring pivotal goals or securing game-changing assists in every match. At the 2019 FIFA Women's World Cup, she scored twice in the quarter final against France. A hamstring injury forced her to sit out for the semi-finals but she bounced back to steal the show in the final, scoring her 50th international goal in a penalty kick.

Going beyond her talent on the pitch, Megan's activism is one of the things that makes her a true icon. She uses her platform to speak up on the topics of LGBTQ rights, racism and equal pay. Go, Megan.

HER AWESOME ACHIEVEMENTS

➜ The fourth ever woman to win *Sports Illustrated*'s Sportsperson of the Year in the award's 66-year history.

➜ Became co-captain of the US women's national team in 2018, alongside Carli Lloyd and Alex Morgan.

➜ Was crowned Best FIFA Women's Player and awarded the Golden Boot for being top scorer and the Golden Ball award for best player in 2019.

➜ Unanimously voted Outsports' Person of the Decade in 2020 for being an outspoken advocate for LGBTQ rights, equal pay, transgender rights and youth.

"IF EVERYBODY WAS AS OUTRAGED BY HOMOPHOBIA AS THE LGBTQ PLAYERS, IF EVERYBODY WAS OUTRAGED ABOUT THE LACK OF EQUAL PAY AND INVESTMENT IN THE WOMEN'S GAME OTHER THAN JUST WOMEN, THAT WOULD BE THE MOST INSPIRING THING TO ME."

MARIEL MARGARET "MIA" HAMM

17 March 1972–Present

HER SUPERPOWERS:

One of the foremost soccer icons, Mia Hamm has made an unforgettable impact on national and international football.

HER INCREDIBLE STORY

With four FIFA Women's World Cups, three Olympics games and an outstanding national career under her belt, Mia Hamm is one of the most capped players in international soccer, with an awe-inspiring 276 appearances.

Mia was born with a club foot and spent most of her early years travelling due to her father's role in the US Air Force. It was when her family moved from Alabama to Florence, Italy, that football came into Mia's life.

On their return to the USA, Mia joined a local Texas football club aged five. Despite being the smallest on her team, she already knew the game inside-out. She'd often be picked last because of her petite frame, but once people saw her lightning speed and athletic agility, perceptions soon changed!

As Mia was growing up, a new regulation – Title IX – was introduced and spurred on many schools to open up their previously male-only sports programmes to women. This led to high schools and colleges offering sports scholarships to women – something that was previously unheard of. In no time at all, Mia went from excelling on boys' teams in junior high to becoming the youngest player to play for the US women's national team in 1987, aged 15.

Over her career, Mia played in four FIFA Women's World Cups (1991, 1995, 1999, 2003) and three Olympic Games (1996, 2000, 2004). She made football history for being on the winning team of the first ever FIFA Women's World Cup in 1991 and part of the first Olympics to feature women's soccer in 1996.

Mia played a total of 43 games and scored 14 goals during her time on the US women's national soccer team, and she navigated the pitch with outstanding grace and pace in every match. She helped her team secure two FIFA Women's World Cup wins and two Olympic golds. In doing so, Mia took women's football to places it had never been before and quickly became the face of the sport in the 1990s and 2000s.

After nearly three decades on the pitch, Mia announced her retirement in 2004. She still plays a very active role in football, as a co-owner of Los Angeles FC, a global ambassador for FC Barcelona and a director for a number of other clubs. Being an icon in women's football, and with two young girls of her own, she's very passionate about gender equality in sports. Mia has spoken out about closing the football gender pay gap and her foundation, the Mia Hamm Foundation, works to drive female participation and stop gender discrimination in sports. What a legend.

HER AWESOME ACHIEVEMENTS

→ Won US Soccer Female Athlete of the Year five times, awarded by the US Soccer Federation.

→ Named Sportswoman of the Year in 1997 and 1999 by the Women's Sports Foundation.

→ Until 2013, Mia held the record for scoring more international goals than any other player (male or female). She still ranks first in the US team's history for assists (144).

→ Became the first woman inducted into the World Football Hall of Fame in 2013.

"MY COACH SAID I RAN LIKE A GIRL. I SAID IF HE COULD RUN A LITTLE FASTER HE COULD TOO."

MICHELLE KWAN

7 JULY 1980–PRESENT

HER SUPERPOWERS:

From Olympic gold figure skater to sports analyst and diplomat, Michelle is all kinds of iconic.

HER INCREDIBLE STORY

Michelle Kwan grew up in a Cantonese-American household in California. From eight years old, she showed the determination of a true athlete. Michelle's dad would hand her $5.75 (the cost of a session on the rink) and, in non-pushy-parent style, give her the choice: "You can either go to the ice rink, or you can go and buy some candy." She chose the ice rink every time, and it paid off.

The more she practised, the more she shone. But as she got better, the need for advanced coaching, costumes and travel got greater. Her parents ran into serious financial hardship trying to cover it all. And with nothing left in the bank, it was all looking hopeless for Michelle until she attracted the attention of a scout at a competition. At ten years old, she was offered a scholarship to train at Ice Castle International Training Centre along with her sister – and just a few years later, she was taking on the world.

Michelle's childhood tenacity stayed with her long into her pro career. When Michelle showed up on the ice, she showed up to win. And win she did. In total, Michelle won 43 championships over the years, including five golds at the World Championships and nine golds at the US Championships – more than any other American skater in history.

In the 1996 World Championships, Michelle beat the defending champion Chen Lu and, at just 15, became the best skater in the world.

Kwan continued to win worldwide and managed to secure a silver (1998) and a bronze (2002) in the Olympics. She became well known as "Silent Blades" for her quiet, graceful technique and is one of the only skaters who can spin in both directions. She'd often land awe-inspiring triple flips and complicated loop combinations with barely a whisper on the ice. She had a unique way of making even the trickiest of moves look effortless in every performance.

Michelle retired in 2006 to focus on her degree and has kept herself very busy since. She's worked as a broadcast analyst for the Winter Olympics and a senior advisor for the state, sharing her passion for public affairs and social change. From white ice to the White House, Michelle's also worked with Obama and Clinton as an envoy. She played a pivotal role on the President's Council on Fitness, Sport and Nutrition, Hillary Clinton's Council to Empower Women and Girls Through Sports, and the Board of Directors of Special Olympics. A trailblazer on and off the ice.

HER AWESOME ACHIEVEMENTS

→ The most decorated figure skater in US history, with 43 championship wins.

→ Named US Olympic Committee's Athlete of the Month 14 times – more than any other athlete, male or female.

→ Appointed as public diplomacy ambassador by the Secretary of State in 2006, travelling widely to inspire young people and sports enthusiasts.

→ Honoured with the "You Bring Charm to the World" award in 2007, for being one of the most influential Chinese people of all time.

"I DIDN'T LOSE GOLD. I WON THE SILVER."

NATALIA PARTYKA

27 JULY 1989-PRESENT

HER SUPERPOWERS:

A Paralympian and Olympian athlete who's achieved incredible things against the odds, Natalia Partyka has her eyes firmly set on gold.

HER INCREDIBLE STORY

Being born without a right hand or forearm has never held Natalia back from achieving exceptional things. At the age of 11, she became the youngest Paralympian of all time when she competed in the table tennis championship. It might have been a history-making moment for the Paralympics, but to Natalia, it was nothing new. She'd been playing table tennis to win since she was seven. Her first match came when she followed her big sister to the table tennis hall in their hometown of Gdansk, Poland. With sibling rivalry at stake, Natalia kept playing until she could beat her sister and just about everyone else around her.

Growing up, Natalia watched other disabled athletes compete from a young age, which helped her feel inspired and believe in her own strength. She learned to balance the ball carefully in the crook of her right elbow, then drop it on the bat and serve with her left hand. This amazing technique has served her well and helped her become one of the most successful Paralympians of all time.

At the age of 15, Natalia won her first gold (and a silver) at the 2004 Athens Paralympics. It was a huge year for her as she also scooped two gold medals at the International Table Tennis Federation's European Championship for Cadets. She continued to serve up medals, winning three golds at the European Paralympic Championships and one at the International Paralympic Committee's Table Tennis World Championships in 2006. And after another year of triple golds at the European Paralympic Championships in 2007, Natalia decided to take on both the Summer Paralympics and the Summer Olympics in 2008.

This wonder woman was one of only two athletes to compete in both the Olympics and the Paralympics in 2008. The other was the similarly named, equally fantastic female athlete Natalie du Toit, who competed in swimming. Natalia won three sets to nil in the 2008 Paralympics and took home another gold. She put up an awesome fight at the Olympics, too, narrowly missing out to world number ten, Tie Yana.

Natalia has since won gold in every Paralympics and continues to work her way up the rankings in the Olympics. While seven-year-old Natalia just wanted to beat her sister at table tennis, she's beaten a world of competition to date and become an amazing role model. And if she can help people see disability differently, that's OK with her: "Maybe someone will see me and realise their own disability is not the end of the world. Maybe sometimes you have to work a little harder if you really want to do something. If I'm an inspiration, I can't complain." What an inspiration she is.

HER AWESOME ACHIEVEMENTS

➔ The youngest ever Paralympian table tennis champion.

➔ Won a total of five golds, two silvers and a bronze at the Paralympics, making her one of the most decorated female Paralympians of all time.

➔ Awarded one of Poland's honours, the Knight's Cross of the Order of Polonia Restituta, for sporting achievement.

➔ Co-initiated Natalia Partyka's Fund to support young athletes who have faced adversities and difficulties in developing their careers.

"I RELY ON MY PERSEVERANCE [AND] HARD WORK, AND I FULLY BELIEVE THAT EVERYTHING IS UP TO ME."

MOKGADI CASTER SEMENYA

7 JANUARY 1991–PRESENT

HER SUPERPOWERS:

The record-breaking, boundary-defying, Olympic-winning runner who's had her gender publicly questioned for years – simply because she is a super-fast runner. Caster Semenya is amazing (exactly as she is).

HER INCREDIBLE STORY

Winning a gold medal at a world-renowned sporting event is an incredible achievement. Beating your personal best is even greater cause for congratulation. Or, at least it should have been for Caster Semenya. But the events following Semenya's win at the 2009 African Junior Championships were far from the celebrations you might expect for a runner who had just broken a world record for the 800-m race.

Instead of being hailed a hero, Semenya was accused of being a fraud. The International Association of Athletics Federation (IAAF) questioned if she was really a woman because of her super-speedy performance and made Semenya take a sex verification test. The results were never published, but in November 2009, the IAAF officially announced that Semenya could keep her medal and award. Shortly after, she was cleared to compete again.

This was a huge ordeal for the 18-year-old to go through. Thankfully, Semenya received overwhelming support across the globe including from South Africa's Minister of Sport and Recreation, Makhenkesi Stofile. This spurred her on to take legal action and she appointed a law firm to protect her human and civil rights.

Refusing to let the negativity get in the way of what she loves most, Semenya has sprinted from success to success since 2009. In 2016, she became the first person to win the 400-m relay and 800-m and 1,500-m titles in the South African Championships. She won gold at the 800-m at the Rio Olympics the same year. Caster Semenya is nothing short of remarkable, but with every victory has come more scrutiny.

In 2018, the IAAF announced a change in rules that meant women with particularly high levels of testosterone would be forced to take medication to lower their levels – or race against men – to compete in the 400-m, 800-m or 1,500-m races. As these are Semenya's famous races, many thought this was directly aimed at her. How did she take the news? With strength and dignity, as ever. Instead of feeling deflated, Semenya took legal action against the IAAF to protect the rights of other women. She's also shared her story through a Nike ad, where she boldly lets the world know that she was "born to do this".

Her determination to see that her (and others') unique genetic gifts are celebrated is unwavering, and Semenya's not giving up the fight. In addition to track, she's turned her attention to football, stating that no human being will stop her from running. Semenya signed to South African team JVW FC in September 2019.

Thank goodness for her tenacity, because the sporting world is a more wonderful place with Semenya in it.

HER AWESOME ACHIEVEMENTS

→ Fourth fastest female 800-m runner of all time, with a personal best of 1:54.25.

→ Included in the *New Statesman*'s list of "50 People Who Matter" in 2010.

→ Awarded South African Sportswoman of the Year at the SA Sports Awards, 2012.

→ Won gold for women's 800 m at the 2016 Olympics in Rio.

→ Appeared in a spotlight feature in Nike's 30th "Just Do It" anniversary campaign in 2018.

"I WANT TO RUN NATURALLY, THE WAY I WAS BORN… I AM MOKGADI CASTER SEMENYA. I AM A WOMAN AND I AM FAST."

NICOLA ADAMS

26 October 1982–present

HER SUPERPOWERS:

An LGBTQ advocate and one of the most successful female boxers of all time, enter the one and only Nicola Adams.

HER INCREDIBLE STORY

The first female boxer to represent England and the first woman to win Olympic gold for boxing, Nicola Adams is the personification of tenacity, and her success is far from coincidental.

Nicola was raised by her mum and attributes her boxing success to her strength. Growing up, things weren't easy. Her father was abusive to the point that Nicola remembers jumping in front of her mum to try to separate them. She begged her mum to leave and, eventually, she did. With two kids to provide for, her mum worked two jobs day and night. It taught Nicola that "if you work hard, you can achieve anything you want to".

Nicola started boxing a couple of years after her father left. She became well known for her sparring talents and took on more advanced matches. She trained tirelessly – but things took a catastrophic turn in 2009. Nicola was on her way to an important fight when she slipped on a boxing bandage and fell down the stairs. Nicola, being Nicola, didn't stay down for long – she picked herself up and headed to the fight. She won the match but, in doing so, she seriously damaged her back and spent the next year out of the ring. She spent months in recovery, living penniless at her mum's house, unable to lift a glass of milk without pain, let alone a boxing glove.

To make matters worse, Nicola's dream of women's boxing being introduced to the Olympics came true while she was out of action. She was devastated. When the Team GB squad selection trials came around, she refused to miss out. She went along and, despite being severely injured, convinced the panel that she'd be squad-ready for the 2012 London Olympics.

Her recovery journey was gruelling, but her hard work paid off, and Nicola Adams became the first ever woman to win an Olympic boxing gold. She defended the title four years later, becoming the first British boxer to hold on to an Olympic title in nearly a century.

Incredible, right? But what's her secret? What keeps a record-breaking boxing champion focused? Chess! Nicola confesses that the strategic nature of playing chess helped keep her focused and aligned with the kind of tactics you need to outsmart your opponent in the ring. Who'd have thought it?

In 2019, after tearing her pupil, Nicola announced that she was retiring from the game – with an undefeated record. She may be hanging up her gloves to put her health first, but Nicola Adams continues to be an influential advocate for the LGBTQ community and an inspiration for young female boxers and athletes everywhere.

HER AWESOME ACHIEVEMENTS

➜ First female boxer to win an Olympic gold.

➜ Received an MBE and OBE for outstanding services to boxing.

➜ Retired in 2019 with an undefeated record, holding the World Boxing Organization's female flyweight title.

➜ Named the most influential LGBT person in Britain by the *Independent* in 2012.

"[FEMALE BOXERS] HAVE COME A LONG WAY. IN THE NINETIES, YOU ONLY EVER SAW WOMEN PARADING AROUND IN HEELS AND A BIKINI HOLDING A SCORECARD. NOW WE'RE OWNING IT."

PAULA RADCLIFFE

17 December 1973–present

HER SUPERPOWERS:

There's only one Paula Radcliffe – the marathon runner who dared to dream that she could and did.

HER INCREDIBLE STORY

She's the record-setting marathon runner who challenged stereotypes. And it all started from the sidelines. At ten years old, Paula went with her father to watch him run the London Marathon. It was the year that Ingrid Kristiansen set a women's world marathon record of 2:21.6. Watching Ingrid overtake most male competitors made Paula think, *I'd love to do that* – and she did.

Decades later, in a moment that shocked the British nation, Paula set the women's world marathon record in 2:15.25 at the 2003 London Marathon. That's under five minutes per mile. During the race, people were convinced she couldn't maintain her speed, but she proved the world wrong. Her secret? Passion, pace and perseverance. In the last 800 m, Paula knew that to break the record she needed to cross the line in under three minutes. She did it in 2:25.

Years earlier, Paula had started competing in the 1,500 m at school and built up to 5,000 m and 10,000 m championships, before moving on to half marathons then marathons. But it wasn't all cheery line crosses and record-breaking; Paula suffered exercise-induced asthma and used to black out. She has also dealt with countless injuries, including one that turned her entire knee black from a clot and abscess. The anti-inflammatory drugs she took for this stopped her being able to digest food and caused dehydration.

Powering through the tough times, Paula became one of the biggest names in marathon running. She has set records on the roads and tracks and doesn't do things by halves. Paula won the London Marathon in 2002, 2003 and 2005, as well as the New York Marathon in 2004, 2007 and 2008, and the Helsinki World Championships in 2005. She also won the 5,000 m in the 2002 Commonwealth Games and was the only woman to win the European Cross-Country Championship twice (1998 and 2003). Paula was a favourite to win the 2004 Olympics marathon but, while training, she was hit by a stone from a passing joyrider's wheel and injured herself. Although she still competed in the race, she was unable to finish.

Paula retired in style after finishing the 2015 London Marathon. But she continues to spend her days inspiring women and young people – including her own little people – to run toward their dreams and set their own limits. When she's not being an ambassador for a number of charities, she's spending time with her family. And she hasn't hung up her running shoes just yet. Paula goes for a daily run after dropping the kids off at school, claiming it's the best way to clear her mind and describing the runner's high as "better than the caffeine high".

HER AWESOME ACHIEVEMENTS

➜ Held the women's world marathon record for 16 years – from 2003 to 2019.

➜ Inducted into the England Athletics Hall of Fame in 2010.

➜ A patron for Asthma UK, helping to promote and fundraise for the charity.

➜ Winner of six world championships and seven big city marathons.

"NEVER SET LIMITS, GO AFTER YOUR DREAMS, DON'T BE AFRAID TO PUSH BOUNDARIES."

RACHAEL HEYHOE FLINT

11 June 1939–18 January 2017

HER SUPERPOWERS:

She put the Women's Cricket World Cup on the map, years before the men's one was even founded – all hail cricket pioneer, Baroness Flint.

HER INCREDIBLE STORY

Rachael Heyhoe Flint was a trailblazer in a time when the common perception of women playing cricket was "like a man trying to knit". Swooping on to the scene with a love of sports, she took that outdated perception and batted it into oblivion (where it belongs).

Rachael refused to let stereotypes get in the way of her love for sports, despite growing up in the 1940–50s. When she was young, a policeman caught her and a group of friends playing cricket in the street and asked for their names and addresses. He completely ignored Rachael, so she probed: "But I was playing, too. Don't you want my name?" He responded: "Girls don't play cricket." How wrong he was. Years later, Rachael was captaining national teams with her fierce right-handed swing.

In 1959, Rachael took time out from her first teaching job to train for her Test debut in Port Elizabeth. Just a few years later, she legendarily hit the first six in a women's Test match at the Oval, London, in 1963. Her stellar performances started to catch attention and more women were coming forward to show their love of the game. Rachael was made captain of the England women's team in 1966. She celebrated by scoring 113 in her first innings at Scarborough.

With support from a friend, Rachael pioneered two team tours to the West Indies before seeding the idea of an inaugural Women's Cricket World Cup in 1973. She worked day and night to organize the event, which was, according to the British media, "made up of four housewives, nine teachers and one secretary". Their hard work paid off and the team won by 92 runs.

Rachael spent a total of 12 years as the England captain, leading the team all over the world. But despite her efforts and talent, not everyone was receptive to her game-changing ways. Marylebone Cricket Club (MCC), known as the Lord's Cricket Ground, rejected Rachael's first request to join in 1991. But she didn't give up, naturally, and was admitted eight years later as one of the club's first ever female members.

Long after her retirement, Rachael's impact on the game was still felt. In 2008, she received the second-highest honours of the British Empire (OBE) for her services to cricket. In 2010, she became the first woman to be inducted into the ICC Cricket Hall of Fame and was appointed Baroness in 2011. Rachael sadly passed away in 2017 but her legacy lives on every year with the Women's Cricket World Cup.

HER AWESOME ACHIEVEMENTS

→ Played as a goalkeeper for England's national hockey team in 1964.

→ Set a record of 1,594 runs, at an average of 45.54, from 22 Tests. Only two other British women have achieved more.

→ Scored over 350 runs in a series twice (356 in 1966 against New Zealand at 71.20 and 350 ten years later against Australia at 87.50).

→ Helped establish the first Women's Cricket World Cup, held two years before there was a Men's Cricket World Cup.

"NOW THE MUMS AND THE DAUGHTERS HAVE THEIR OWN CRICKET, INSTEAD OF MAKING CUCUMBER SANDWICHES EVERY WEEKEND."

RONDA ROUSEY

1 FEBRUARY 1987–PRESENT

HER SUPERPOWERS:

From judo Olympian to World Wrestling Entertainment (WWE) title-holder, Ronda "Rowdy" Rousey is a fighter in and out of the ring.

HER INCREDIBLE STORY

Ronda Rousey is big on firsts. Not only is she the first – and only – woman to win both an Ultimate Fighting Championship (UFC) and WWE championship, she's also the first American woman to win an Olympic medal in judo and the first female fighter be inducted into the UFC Hall of Fame.

After discovering photos of her mum in a judo black belt, Ronda decided to give the sport a go at 11. Judo soon became more than a hobby and turned into a way of dealing with the tough times she'd faced growing up. Ronda had nearly died at birth from umbilical complications. She was left with brain damage that meant she couldn't speak a word until she was six. Then, at eight, her father broke his back while sledding with Ronda and her sisters. His condition regressed and, having been told he had just a few years left to live, he took his own life.

Ronda turned to judo as an outlet for her grief. After winning countless championships, she became the youngest judo athlete to qualify for the 2004 Olympic Games in Athens at just 17. She lost her first match to silver medal winner Claudia Heill but came back fighting in the 2008 Olympics and took home bronze.

At 21, Ronda decided to switch judo for mixed martial arts (MMA). She moved to Venice Beach, California, to pursue the sport and worked three jobs to support herself (and her dog). Training in between shifts, Ronda remembers going home crying most nights after getting thrown around. But she didn't give in – even when people told her she was "too pretty to get hit in the face and should go back to judo". She had her first MMA fight in 2010 and defeated Hayden Munoz in 23 seconds.

Ronda persevered with bantamweight MMA and became the first female fighter to sign with the UFC in 2012. She was also one of the very first women to compete in pay-per-view UFC fights, defending her Bantamweight Women's Champion title in a number of nail-biting matches. She faced possibly the biggest fight of her career in 2014, when she took on Olympic medallist and undefeated winner Sara McMann. It was Ronda's first win by knockout and she was crowned winner in under a minute.

Ronda's three-year reign came to an end in 2015 when she lost her fight to Holly Holm. But she didn't stay out of the ring long. She signed with WWE in 2017 and soon became their second-longest-standing Raw Women's champion.

Ronda's story defines why our past doesn't have to determine our future and the power of finding positive ways to battle through grief and hardship. We salute you, Ronda.

HER AWESOME ACHIEVEMENTS

➜ First American woman to win an Olympic medal in judo.

➜ Sixth-degree judo black belt, with eight USA Judo medals from the US Opens and two from USA Fall Classic.

➜ Won the first ever women's fight in UFC history and has achieved the most title defences by a woman in UFC history.

➜ First Mixed Martial Artist to win an ESPY award (2014).

"ONE OF THE GREATEST DAYS OF MY LIFE WAS WHEN I CAME TO UNDERSTAND THAT OTHER PEOPLE'S APPROVAL AND MY HAPPINESS WERE NOT RELATED."

SAINA NEHWAL

17 MARCH 1990–PRESENT

HER SUPERPOWERS:

*Badminton star Saina Nehwal dominated the court
to become one of the most successful sportspeople
in India – and all before she turned 30.*

HER INCREDIBLE STORY

Saina Nehwal doesn't believe in tricks or untoward tactics. Her immediate focus on the badminton court is to overpower her opponent, studying their strengths and style so she can tailor hers to beat them. It's that focus and technique that has seen Saina go from shy schoolgirl to world-leading badminton champion in a matter of years.

When Saina first picked up a racquet, she was looking for friendships not championships. Her family had moved from Haryana to Hyderabad in India and, as Saina didn't speak the local language, she started playing badminton to meet other kids. It changed from a hobby to making history in 2006, when Saina became the first player to win the Asian Satellite Badminton tournament twice and was crowned under-19 champion at just 16. The very same year, she defeated the then world number four Xu Huaiwen and Julia Wong Pei Xian, and became the first Indian woman and youngest Asian player to win a four-star tournament at the Philippines Open.

For her entire career, Saina has been a player of many firsts. In 2008, she was crowned the first Indian person to win the World Junior Badminton Championships and also became the first Indian woman to reach the quarter finals at the Olympics.

One of her proudest career moments came at the 2010 Commonwealth Games, when she won gold in the Women's Singles. Saina found herself a match-point down in the second set but managed to make an incredible comeback in a challenging game against Wong Mew Choo. She won 19–21, 23–21, 21–13 and became the first Indian person to win a Commonwealth gold in badminton. She then shuttled her way to a second one in 2018.

Saina was ranking fifth in the world when she headed to the 2012 London Olympics. At the games, she celebrated her way through group stages before coming up against a strong opponent, Yao Jie, in the knockouts. She excelled with straight game wins and got to the quarter finals. Saina took home bronze, landing India its first ever Olympic medal in badminton.

Not disheartened by missing out on gold, Saina worked her socks off and, in 2015, she achieved her dream of being ranked world number one for badminton. It was a moment that made history – she was the first Indian women to achieve the ranking and only the second Indian sportsperson ever. In a country where only a handful of women achieve global sporting success, Saina's achievements are no mean feat. They're testament to her work ethic, which includes eight hours' training per day.

Recently, Saina's been working hard towards a very different kind of first, as she ventures into the world of politics.

HER AWESOME ACHIEVEMENTS

→ First female badminton player from India to be ranked world number one.

→ The only Indian sportsperson to have won at least one medal in every Badminton World Federation (BWF) major individual event – the Olympics, the BWF World Championships and the BWF Junior Championships.

→ A passionate philanthropist, Saina was ranked 18th most charitable athlete in 2015.

"I BECAME WORLD NUMBER ONE, NOT ONCE, NOT TWICE, BUT THRICE. I SLIPPED AND GOT BACK AGAIN. I SLIPPED AND GOT BACK AGAIN. WHAT MORE CAN I ASK FOR?"

SARAH STOREY

26 October 1977–present

HER SUPERPOWERS:

There's multi-talented and then there's Sarah Storey. The most successful British Paralympian in history, Sarah Storey is a champion cyclist and swimmer in both Paralympic and non-disabled championships.

HER INCREDIBLE STORY

From water to track and road, Sarah has defined inspirational by winning 14 Paralympic golds and becoming one of the most successful Paralympians of all time.

Being born without a functioning left arm has only ever made Sarah more determined to succeed. She grew up in Manchester, UK, in an active family, and from a young age she wanted to "do every single sport". She learned to swim aged four and her childhood Saturdays would often start with an early morning swim, followed by a muddy cross-country run, a quick shower and then an afternoon table tennis tournament.

But with the adrenaline-fuelled highs came emotional lows. The more successful Sarah got, the harder her time at school became. After she won her first Paralympic medals in swimming races (two golds, three silvers and a bronze) aged just 14, in 1992, many of Sarah's classmates became jealous and started to isolate her, and she was dropped from being netball captain. She would sit in the toilets listening to people say horrible things about her and stopped eating to avoid the lunchtime nastiness.

It was her love of sports and parental support that got Sarah through the bullying. And by the time she hit 18, she'd won another three Paralympic golds.

After stellar Paralympics swimming performances, Sarah decided to try a new sport around 2004 due to continued ear infections from the water. She'd always enjoyed riding a bike but initially worried that people would think she "didn't have enough of a disability" to compete in Paralympic cycling. It took teams of professionals to explain that cycling success was about much more than having two legs. Only having one functioning arm significantly affects Sarah's balance, but that didn't stop her from winning the 2008 Paralympics individual cycling pursuit – with a time fit for the Olympic top eight – in her first year of competing.

Sarah went on to win four golds in the time trial, individual pursuit and road race in the 2012 Paralympics. She then won a further three golds in the 3,000-m individual pursuit, time trial and road race in 2016. Not limiting herself to Paralympic championships, Sarah has also won medals in non-disabled national track competitions, including two pursuits, one points race and three team pursuits. She took on the gruelling hour record in 2015 and epically set the British and C5 Paralympic record with a distance of 45.502 km.

When Sarah isn't lapping the track, she's often running around after her children or raising money for the breast cancer charity that supported her mother. She's a living lesson in the importance of not letting people's opinions hold you back from achieving your dreams.

HER AWESOME ACHIEVEMENTS

→ The most decorated British Paralympian in history, with 14 gold medals.

→ A world champion 29 times (23 in cycling and six in swimming), a European champion 21 times (18 in swimming and three in cycling) and holder of 75 world records.

→ The first English disabled cyclist to compete against non-disabled cyclists in the Commonwealth Games.

→ Appointed Dame Commander of the Order of the British Empire (DBE) in 2013.

"DON'T PUT ANY LIMITS ON YOURSELF. PEOPLE, EXTERNAL INFLUENCES WILL TRY TO PERSUADE YOU INTO OTHER DIRECTIONS BUT I BELIEVE THERE ARE NO SUCH THINGS AS BOUNDARIES."

SERENA WILLIAMS

26 September 1981–present

HER SUPERPOWERS:

Sports superstar, role model, ambassador. She's been called the greatest tennis player of all time and it all started with two sisters, a racket and one big dream.

HER INCREDIBLE STORY

It's hard to imagine the tennis world without Serena Williams. With 23 major singles titles under her belt, Serena has won more than any other man or women in the Open Era and has been ranked number one by the World Tennis Association eight times.

Dominating the international tennis scene for decades, Serena has torn up the court as awesomely alone as she has with her sister. She's earned 72 championship titles, landed a breathtaking number of Grand Slams and won four Olympic golds. And, thankfully, she shows no signs of slowing down.

What's her secret? Technically, Serena is a baseline player. This gives her time and space to assess and react to her opponent's shots. Her two-handed backhand and fierce forehand strokes are both delivered powerfully, and her iconic power serve is known as one of the greatest in tennis history. In fact, her peak serve speed is the third fastest of all time amongst female players.

Some call her style "high risk" because there is no hesitation, no jerking or jittering, just maximum pace and power. This enables Serena to take control of rallies quickly and excel at both offence and defence, whether she's on clay, grass or sand.

She might make it look effortless but Serena has been perfecting her tennis technique from a young age. Her first tennis game was at four years old, when her mother and father became Serena and

Venus' official coaches. She started at the tennis academy of Rick Macci with her sister at nine and, by the age of ten, Serena was ranked number one amongst players under ten in Florida.

One of Serena's most inspirational traits is her ability to bounce back from loss, adversity and judgement. From her early years in tennis, Serena has faced racism and negativity. For 14 years, the Williams family all boycotted the Indian Wells tournament after the crowd jeered and made racist comments to her dad while Serena played in 2001. She's been illustrated as an angry black monster numerous times for daring to speak her mind. She's had her comfortable tennis outfits banned in favour of traditional tiny tennis skirts. And she's constantly told she's "too big" for having muscles that men would be praised for.

But the more people have tried to bring her down, the taller she has stood and the harder she has fought. To this day, Serena uses her platform to invoke change and regularly speaks out about important injustices like inequality, the sports gender pay gap, racism and the media's one-dimensional portrayal of beautiful. What a hero.

HER AWESOME ACHIEVEMENTS

→ Ranked world number one singles player eight separate times between 2002 and 2017 by the Women's Tennis Association.

→ First African American to win the Australian Open, in 2003.

→ Seven times Wimbledon singles champion.

→ Has broken records as the only tennis player to ever complete the career Grand Slam over the age of 30.

→ Won a Grand Slam title on every surface (hard, clay and grass) in one calendar year.

"PEOPLE CALL ME ONE OF THE 'WORLD'S GREATEST FEMALE ATHLETES'. DO THEY SAY LEBRON IS ONE OF THE WORLD'S BEST MALE ATHLETES? IS TIGER? FEDERER? WHY NOT? WE SHOULD NEVER LET THIS GO UNCHALLENGED. WE SHOULD ALWAYS BE JUDGED BY OUR ACHIEVEMENTS, NOT OUR GENDER."

SIMONE BILES

14 MARCH 1997–PRESENT

HER SUPERPOWERS:

At 142 cm, Simone Biles defied every stereotype about strength and stature when she vaulted, flew, beamed and leaped her way to five Olympic medals in her debut year at the games.

HER INCREDIBLE STORY

Before 2016, you could be forgiven for not knowing the name "Simone Biles". But when the Texan gymnast sauntered onto the 2016 Rio Olympics stage, she instantly became an icon.

For many years, gymnastics has been somewhat outshone by the split-second track races of the Olympics. Simone played a big part in changing that in 2016, when she took to the floor with a show-stopping routine to defend Team USA's gymnastics title.

Growing up in and out of foster care, Simone had never imagined Olympic fame. But seeing the US gymnastics team, "the Fierce Five", win gold in London 2012 made Simone think *perhaps I can be there myself one day.* Flip forward four years and there she was, stacking up 15.800 points in her debut floor performance and landing her first Olympic gold of many.

But Simone's journey into gymnastics was far from planned or privileged. Aged six years old, she was on a day care field trip when she wandered into a gym area and peeked at a team tumbling and flipping. She started copying the older gymnasts' moves so impressively that the coach sent a letter home to her grandparents asking them to let her train. She enrolled in gymnastics shortly after and was coached by Aimee Boorman from eight years old.

Simone's junior career started at 14 and, after a rocky start, she worked her way up to her first gold medal in vault in 2012. She joined the US Junior National Team later that year.

In her senior international debut Simone showed what a world class act she was, winning two golds (floor and individual all-around), a silver in vault and a bronze on the beam at the 2013 World Championships. She suffered an injury shortly afterwards but bounced back to win another four golds at the 2014 World Championships. A year later, she was the first African-American woman to win the all-round title and became the USA's most decorated female at the World Championships.

For someone so young who'd been in foster care just a decade before, Simone Biles' 2016 Olympic performance was a breathtaking storm. Even when she slipped slightly on the balance beam on day two and fell from first to third in the competition, she managed to claw back the lead and finish up on the highest podium place.

Simone took a break from gymnastics in 2017 to focus on other projects, before making an incredible comeback in the US Classic, where she scored 58.700 – the highest score recorded in three years. She has since spoken out about big topics like racism and sexual abuse, proving that she's one of the biggest inspirations of this generation.

HER AWESOME ACHIEVEMENTS

→ The most decorated gymnast in the USA and the third most decorated gymnast in the world, with 30 medals.

→ Holds the record for the most World Championship medals won by a gymnast of any gender.

→ Awarded Team USA Female Olympic Athlete of the Year in December 2015, as only the fourth gymnast to win the accolade.

→ Took home four Olympic golds at the 2016 Rio Olympics, in team, all-around, beam and vault.

"I'M NOT THE NEXT USAIN BOLT OR MICHAEL PHELPS: I'M THE FIRST SIMONE BILES."

STEPHANIE GILMORE

29 JANUARY 1988–PRESENT

HER SUPERPOWERS:

Surf is always up for smiling superstar Stephanie Gilmore. With a record seven world titles to her name, she's one of the greatest surfers in history.

HER INCREDIBLE STORY

They don't call her "Happy Gilmore" for nothing. Australian Stephanie Gilmore might be one of the world's most successful female surfers, but you wouldn't know it from her down-to-earth, humble demeanour.

When Stephanie secured her seventh world title in 2018, she made history with the biggest smile on her face and sincerely thanked the female surfers who'd inspired her along the way. Throughout the championship, her paddling strength and surf lines were, as ever, impeccable. And it's that skill and unrivalled love of the ocean that has kept her teetering at the top of the rankings for the last decade.

However, Stephanie's path to success hasn't been without stress. In 2011, she was forced to take an unwanted break from surfing after being attacked by a man with a metal bar in the stairwell to her apartment. She spent seven weeks recovering and missed out on a number of competitions. It left her with both physical and emotional scars but made her even more determined to get back into the ocean – the second home that she's loved since she first jumped on a board at ten years old. She made an incredible comeback, landing a World Surf League (WSL) title a year later in 2012 and another one in 2014.

While the image of surfing and Stephanie's personality might be laid back, her training routine is anything but. Riding hugely powerful, often unpredictable waves for hours at a time takes extremely high levels of stamina. The manoeuvres require plenty of squats and twists, calling for a mixture of strength and athleticism. When not in the ocean, Stephanie spends her days doing running sprints, leg presses, hot power yoga and other hardcore training routines.

Dedicated coaching and training helped fuel her 2018 record victory, and what made it so special was that she hadn't won at the WSL for a few years. She'd admittedly started to lose confidence, but dipping down the ranks helped her to see how much competing meant to her. With that, she came back fighting – and landed a record win – in the year of her 30th birthday. It was the same year that the decision was made for professional female surfers to be paid the same as professional male surfers. High fives all around.

Stephanie invests time and effort in helping to protect the oceans and seas. She's travelled the world working on projects to help ensure everyone has access to fresh water and she supports campaigns to clean up our oceans and look after their wildlife. With the world as her oyster, she continues to show girls that surfing definitely isn't a man's world.

HER AWESOME ACHIEVEMENTS

→ Seven-time women's world surfing champion and joint record holder.

→ The first ever surfer to win a world title as a rookie.

→ The first ever surfer to win championships in every one of their first four seasons on tour (2007–2010).

→ Awarded the Laureus World Sports Award, thought of as the most prestigious award in action sports, in 2010.

"THE OCEAN HUMBLES YOU. YOU CAN GO AND WIN A WORLD TITLE, BUT YOU'RE NEVER GOING TO BEAT THE OCEAN."

STEPHANIE HOUGHTON

23 APRIL 1988–PRESENT

HER SUPERPOWERS:

She started football in the playground with a love of "beating the boys". Decades later, that passion has helped Stephanie Houghton put women's football firmly on the international map.

HER INCREDIBLE STORY

Coming from a sporty family, Stephanie had a ball at her feet as soon as she could walk. Her school days' breaks and lunches were spent entangled in five-a-side kick-arounds with the boys, and it wasn't long before she moved up from playground league.

After a summer coaching school with UK-based Sunderland FC, Steph wowed the team and officially became a Sunderland player aged 14. In her five years there, she helped the team get promoted and won FA Young Player of the Year in 2007. Her talent attracted attention and, when Sunderland were relegated, she reluctantly realized that it was time for a new challenge. Steph was initially torn between Arsenal and Leeds but decided that Leeds was the best choice for her. She joined Leeds United Ladies FC in the summer of 2007.

As her national career levelled up, Steph set her eyes on international football. Her dreams came true when she was called up to the England squad in 2007. It was one of the proudest days of her life. Steph made it all the way to China for the 2007 World Cup, ready to make her debut as the squad's youngest player. But her dreams were shattered when a strength coach confirmed she'd broken her leg during training and there was no way she could compete. The cup curse continued when she was forced to miss the Euros in 2009 due to a damaged ligament.

Her luck finally turned around in 2012 when she was called up for the first Great Britain women's Olympic football team, where she aced three goals playing as a left-back. Two years later, Steph was made captain of the England women's team and her World Cup moment came in 2015. She netted a stunning goal against Norway, was awarded Player of the Match and helped the team qualify for the first ever semi-final and go on to win bronze. Her club career has been just as special as her international one. After leaving Leeds, Steph spent a brief period at Arsenal where she championed the power of twos – helping the team win two Women's Super League (WSL) titles, two FA Cups and two FA WSL Continental Cups. She then went on to Man City FC, where she won the county cup twice, plus the WSL and the FA Cup.

Steph surpassed her 100th international appearance, captaining the "Lionesses" in the 2019 FIFA World Cup. Not only was it an incredible personal achievement, the tournament was a game-changer. It highlighted the sheer skill and level of talent in women's football. Steph continues to use her platform for a great cause, helping girls and women get into the game and being an ambassador for ending period poverty.

HER AWESOME ACHIEVEMENTS

→ Over 100 England caps since her debut in 2007.

→ Became the UK women's team's record left-back goal scorer in the 2012 Olympics, scoring in all three game groups.

→ Appointed Member of the Order of the British Empire (MBE) in 2016 for her services to football.

→ Ambassador or patron for many charities, actively helping to support young people and causes close to her heart.

"I ALWAYS REMEMBER MY SECONDARY SCHOOL PE TEACHER TOLD ME I'D NEVER PLAY FOR ENGLAND... SOME PEOPLE MIGHT HAVE STOPPED PLAYING BECAUSE OF THAT COMMENT, BUT IT MADE ME MORE DETERMINED TO PROVE HER WRONG AND HELPED DRIVE ME TO BE WHERE I AM NOW."

TANNI GREY-THOMPSON

26 JULY 1969–PRESENT

HER SUPERPOWERS:

As one of the most decorated and influential Paralympians of all time, Tanni Grey-Thompson doesn't just believe that anything is possible, she has shown that it is.

HER INCREDIBLE STORY

Right from her school years, Tanni refused to let anyone else define what she could and couldn't do. She saw having spina bifida and being in a wheelchair as just a part of who she was – and she wasn't willing to let it limit her achievements. Tanni found her love of wheelchair racing at 13, and by the age of 17 she'd become part of the British Wheelchair Racing Squad.

In the background of her early success, Tanni underwent life-saving surgery when she had a metal rod grafted to her spine to hold it straight. But in true Tanni style, she was back to training for her first Paralympics (1988 in Seoul) before long. She brought home bronze for her performance in the 400 m but was forced to go back to hospital shortly afterwards, when the metal rod snapped out of her back during training. Tanni was bed-bound for months but made an incredible comeback in the 1992 Paralympics in Barcelona. She wowed the world by winning four golds in the 100-m, 200-m, 400-m and 800-m wheelchair races and silver in the 4 x 100-m relay. The very same year, she won her first London Marathon Wheelchair race – a medal she defended six times in her career.

It was the start of an epic decade for Tanni Grey-Thompson – one in which she established herself as a Paralympic legend. Dominating all wheelchair races in the Paralympics, she took home a total of

11 golds, four silvers and a bronze between 1992 and 2004. That's on top of five golds, four silvers and three bronzes at the World Championships. She also broke an astonishing 30 world records along the way.

In the same way that she's more than just her disability, Tanni is more than just an athlete. Over the last decades, she has used her platform to become a powerful voice for disability rights and gender equality. She has supported National Disability Council, the Sports Council for Wales, UK Sport and the National Lottery panel, helping to make sure decisions don't overlook the diverse needs of people with disabilities.

Since retiring in 2007, Tanni has focused her energy on squashing misconceptions about disability and campaigning to change societal attitudes towards disabled people. One of Tanni's biggest inspirations was seeing someone in a wheelchair complete the London Marathon and thinking "I want to do that". She's done "that" and so much more. From earning her place in sporting history to taking up her place in politics and campaigning for positive change, Tanni Grey-Thompson defines the word "icon".

HER AWESOME ACHIEVEMENTS

→ Won a total of 28 international medals for wheelchair racing across the Paralympic Games and World Championships.

→ Promoted from MBE to OBE to DBE (Dame Commander of the British Empire) for her services to sport in 2000 and 2005 respectively.

→ Named as one of the most powerful women in Britain by BBC *Woman's Hour* in 2013.

→ Works as the patron, president or trustee on more than ten charities and worthy causes.

"ANYTHING IS POSSIBLE. PART OF IT IS HOW MUCH YOU WANT TO DO IT."

TESSA SANDERSON

14 MARCH 1956–PRESENT

HER SUPERPOWERS:

Track and field queen Tessa Sanderson was the first British black woman to win Olympic gold.

HER INCREDIBLE STORY

Trading in the tropics of the Caribbean for the English city of Wolverhampton might not seem like the easiest move in the world, but Tessa Sanderson took it, quite literally, in her stride. She settled into Midlands life by throwing herself into sports.

Athletics became her favourite hobby and it wasn't long before she was wowing mums and dads in school competitions. As a teen, Tessa joined the Wolverhampton & Bilston Athletic Club and became their star javelin thrower and pentathlete. She set a number of junior records before being entered into bigger competitions.

As her sporting success was hitting new heights, Tessa was enduring vile racism in her local area. She remembers being spat on and called a "golliwog" and the n-word. It was incredibly hurtful, but she didn't let people's ignorance and racist views hold her back from doing what she loved.

In 1976, she represented Great Britain in the javelin at the Olympic Games in Montreal. She finished tenth and was the youngest competitor to reach the finals. Her performance just kept getting better and better and, in 1978, she became the first British woman to win the javelin event at the Commonwealth Games in 16 years, out-throwing her competition by 7 metres. She won gold at the Commonwealth Games again in 1986 and 1990.

Never one to shy away from a sporting challenge, Tessa competed in every Olympics between 1976 and 1996. Her dreams came true in 1984, when she became the first black British woman to win Olympic gold – and the only British person to win an Olympic gold for javelin.

Tessa retired from competing in 1997, but she has been heavily involved in sports ever since. For years, she built, grew and ran the Newham Sports Academy in London that helped athletes train to compete in Olympic and Paralympic games. She also served as Vice Chairperson of Sport England and founded her own charity, the Tessa Sanderson Foundation and Academy, to help young disabled and non-disabled athletes achieve their sporting goals.

These are just a few of the many things she's given back to the community she cares deeply about and it hasn't gone unnoticed. This six-time Olympian has gone from MBE to OBE to CBE and even snapped up the *Sunday Times* Lifetime Achievement Award.

Showing true dedication to her love of sports, even Tessa's wedding was a sport-star studded event! She married judo champion Densign White in 2010, with her Olympic teammates Sharron Davies, Kelly Holmes and Christine Ohuruogu as her bridesmaids. Shortly after, in 2013, the couple adopted twins Cassius and Ruby Mae. Who knows, perhaps there are two new javelin-judo Olympians in the making...

HER AWESOME ACHIEVEMENTS:

→ Won gold at three Commonwealth Games (1978, 1986, 1990).

→ First black woman to win an Olympic gold, Los Angeles 1984.

→ Received an MBE, OBE and most recently, in 2004, a CBE for her sports and charity work.

→ Remains the only British javelin thrower to win Olympic gold.

"I STILL SEE MY FIRST THROWS. I FEEL THE FEELING. IT WILL NEVER LEAVE ME."

VENUS WILLIAMS

17 JUNE 1980–PRESENT

HER SUPERPOWERS:

Three times number one female tennis player in the world and one half of the most iconic sporting sisters on the planet, the undeniably epic Venus Williams.

HER INCREDIBLE STORY

The first African-American woman to reach number one in the Open Era, the pioneer who led the fight for equal pay for female tennis professionals and a five-time Olympic medallist, Venus Williams is an outstanding tennis player and so much more.

The elder sister of the Williams duo, Venus was barely in double digits when she hit serve speeds of 100 mph and was ranked number one under-12 female player in Southern California. A driven baseliner, she shattered all stereotypes about women's tennis with her strong attacking serve and exceptional court coverage. This instant superstar brought a level of power to women's tennis that had hardly been seen before.

After a string of successes in the Open Era throughout the 1990s, Venus took home two golds in the 2000 Olympic Games: one in singles and another with her sister in the doubles. It was the start of an iconic reign in both. In total, Venus has won nearly 50 single titles, including seven Grand Slams, and over 13 doubles (with three of those being Olympic golds).

In 2011, Venus was diagnosed with an autoimmune disease that caused significant joint pain and fatigue. She took some time out, changed her diet to vegan and focused on her health before making a comeback in 2012. That year, she and Serena volleyed their way to their 13th Grand Slam and won another epic Olympic Gold.

Such comebacks have been a constant theme in Venus' career. Her glittering record hasn't been without losses. The Williams sisters missed out on an Olympic gold medal at Rio 2016 and Venus has had her fair share of singles defeats. What makes her a true champion is her incredible ability to bounce back and learn from lulls. It's that determination that saw Venus become one of the oldest players to ever take on Wimbledon in 2016, aged 36.

Of all the wins, the title Venus holds closest to her heart is "role model". In 2006, she led a campaign against Wimbledon for "being on the wrong side of history" by refusing to pay men and women equal prize money. Venus fought tirelessly for change and it finally paid off in 2007 when Wimbledon announced they'd be paying equal prize money to all competitors, regardless of gender. The French Open followed suit the next day. Deservedly, Venus was one of the first to benefit from the change when she won the 2007 Wimbledon tournament and received the same prize money as Roger Federer. She has also led the way with the World Tennis Association's partnership with UNESCO, promoting gender equality across the world. An amazing tennis player and an awesome humanitarian, what's not to love?

HER AWESOME ACHIEVEMENTS

→ Holds the record for playing more Grand Slam singles than any other tennis player, male or female, with over 80 match plays.

→ Held the record for the fastest women's serve (129 mph) in 2008, and in three Grand Slam tournaments: the 2007 US Open, the 2007 French Open and Wimbledon 2008.

→ Holds the joint record for most Olympic medals won by a male or female tennis player.

→ Ranked world number one on three occasions by the Women's Tennis Association.

"YOU CAN BE ANYTHING YOU WANT TO BE, AS A MALE OR FEMALE. THAT'S WHAT THIS MESSAGE IS."

WILMA RUDOLPH

23 June 1940–12 November 1994

HER SUPERPOWERS:

From a "sickly child" with a leg brace to the first American woman to win three Olympic golds in track and field, Wilma Rudolph was an extraordinary inspiration.

HER INCREDIBLE STORY

To say that Wilma Rudolph defied the odds would be an understatement. Growing up wearing a leg brace, she was taunted endlessly by other children for not being able to run around and play like they could. Back in the 1940s, in Clarksville, Tennessee, there was very little medical care available to African-American people, so Wilma and her mother were forced to travel 80 km by bus for treatment to help her regain use of her leg.

But this is far from being a sob story – Wilma and her family were determined to make the most of her life. They learned to administer orthopaedic massages four times a day and eventually the treatments started to pay off. Aged 13, Wilma traded her leg brace for an orthopaedic shoe and discovered her love of sports. She decided to try basketball and eventually built up enough strength to play without the orthopaedic shoe. Wilma earned the nickname "Skeeter" for her fast footwork – skills that didn't go unnoticed by local track and field scout Ed Temple. He invited tenth-grade Wilma to join his summer training programme at Tennessee State University and she jumped at the chance.

In her first competitive races at an Amateur Athletic Union, Wilma won all nine of the events she entered. She ran so fast, in fact, that she qualified for Olympic trials. She stormed onto the Olympic scene at just 16, competing in the 200-m individual preliminary heat and the 4 x 100-m relay at the 1956 Melbourne Olympics. Wilma was the youngest in the US team but still helped them bring home bronze for relay.

Wilma gave birth to her daughter, Yolanda, in 1958 but continued to study and train. The 1960 Rome Olympics was everything she'd been waiting for. She set a world record of 23.2 seconds in the 200 m opening heat and went on to compete in the 100-m, 200-m and 4 x 100-m events, winning gold in every one. She became the first American woman to win three Olympic golds and was hailed as the "fastest woman in history".

In a time of racial tension, Wilma's homecoming ceremony was one of the first non-segregated events in Clarksville's history. She used her platform to continue to campaign for desegregation. Her efforts worked and, in 1963, the mayor announced that all public facilities in Clarksville would be open to all.

Wilma retired at the peak of her career, directly after her stellar Olympic performance. She spent her post-athletic days teaching in schools and coaching children on the track, as well as raising children of her own. A game-changer through and through, Wilma also set up her own not-for-profit organization to help underprivileged children into sports. She sadly lost her life to cancer in 1994, but she left an incredible legacy.

HER AWESOME ACHIEVEMENTS

→ The first American woman to win three gold medals in the same Olympic Games.

→ Pioneered desegregation in Clarksville, Tennessee.

→ Founded the Wilma Rudolph Foundation, which continues to help budding young athletes get into sports.

→ The first woman to receive the National Collegiate Athletic Association's Silver Anniversary Award.

"THE TRIUMPH CAN'T BE HAD WITHOUT THE STRUGGLE."

FURTHER READING

My Life: Queen of the Court
Serena Williams
(Simon & Schuster, 2010)

Tessa: My Life in Athletics
Tessa Sanderson
(Willow Books, 1986)

Believe: Boxing, Olympics and My Life Outside the Ring
Nicola Adams
(Viking, 2017)

The Proudest Blue: A Story of Hijab and Family
Ibtihaj Muhammad
(Little Brown Young Readers, 2019)

Aim High
Tanni Grey-Thompson
(Accent Press, 2017)

Sisters
Venus & Serena Williams
(Beach Lane Books, 2019)

Courage to Soar
Simone Biles
(Zondervan, 2018)

Playing to Win
Saina Nehwal
(Penguin Books, 2012)

My Fight, Your Fight
Ronda Rousey
(Century, 2015)

Paula: My Story So Far
Paula Radcliffe
(Simon & Schuster, 2005)

Evie's Magic Bracelet series
Jessica Ennis-Hill
(Hodder Children's Books, 2017)

Pressure is a Privilege: Lessons I've Learned from Life and the Battle of the Sexes
Billie Jean King
(Lifetime Media, 2008)

Have you enjoyed this book?
If so, why not write a review on
your favourite website?

If you're interested in finding out more about
our books, find us on Facebook at **Summersdale
Publishers**, on Twitter at **@Summersdale** and
on Instagram at **@summersdalebooks** and
get in touch. We'd love to hear from you!

Thanks very much for buying
this Summersdale book.

www.summersdale.com